DEDICATION

There's an old saying that states, "Action speaks louder than words." Hal Donaldson, I cannot think of anyone who exemplifies that statement in their personal life more than you. Over the years I have been honored to watch you lead Convoy of Hope with integrity and honesty and your personal life with authenticity and transparency.

You have shaped my leadership, impacted my spiritual life, and challenged my heart more times than I could possibly remember. You are one of the few people I know who possesses the kind of Godly character that could say as the Apostle Paul said, "Follow me, as I follow Christ." I dedicate this book to you Hal, my friend and kingdom partner.

WHAT PEOPLE ARE SAYING
ABOUT *TRACTION*

No traction—no movement. In his latest book *Traction*, my friend Chris Sonksen puts his finger on what every church yearns for—movement. His love for Pastors and His Church, combined with his decades of Pastoring and helping Pastors and churches, makes this book indispensable. Thoughtful. Pragmatic. Instructive. Inspirational. Encouraging. You will share this book with all the leaders you love.

—*Sam Chand*
Leadership Consultant and author of Leadership Pain

Traction is everything! It gives you the speed and momentum to experience the breakthrough you seek. In his latest book, my friend and author, Chris Sonksen lays out the five proven principles that will help your church move quickly towards unstoppable growth. Read the book, apply the principles and watch what happens.

—*Mark Cole*
CEO, The John Maxwell Co.

Traction is one of the best, most helpful, clearly written, and practical church growth books I've read. My friend and author of this book, Chris Sonksen, has used these processes and strategies to coach hundreds of churches to a much greater level of Kingdom success than they could have achieved on their own. It's filled with stories of real churches and the challenges they faced with the practical exercises that helped them break through to new levels of health and growth.

Pastors are God's gift to the church. Their spiritual, emotional, and physical health are critical for the church's missional effectiveness. *Traction* is a great resource that assists pastors in gaining and sustaining ministry momentum.

If there's one guy who can speak to this topic right now in the church world, it's Chris Sonksen! He knows the church and how to take them from where they are and get them moving again into their full God potential!

TRACTION

FIVE PROVEN PRINCIPLES FOR UNSTOPPABLE GROWTH

CHRIS SONKSEN

AVAIL

ISBN: 978-1-962401-33-3   1 2 3 4 5 6 7 8 9 10

Printed in the United States of America

CONTENTS

ACKNOWLEDGMENTS

I would like to thank the following people who through their encouragement and faith in me have helped my personal life and ministry gain traction.

My wife Laura—You often have more confidence in me than I do in myself. You truly make me better. I love you!

My children—Grace, Aidan, Christian, and Katie. Each of you holds a very special place in my heart. May your life forever be dedicated to Jesus and may you find the never-ending traction that will lead you to continual success.

My grandchildren—Mila Brave and Ella Grace—You shine so much light in my life and bring me abundant joy. Papa loves you "this" much.

The Lead Team of Church Boom—I am so grateful for each of you and humbled to call you partners in his work. Let's continue to impact eternity by coaching pastors and rescuing churches.

The team at Four Rivers Media—Thanks for bringing this project to life. You truly gave this book traction.

To my personal coaches—Sam Chand, Dan Reiland, and Eddie Rentz. Your insights, wisdom, and knowledge continually provide fuel for my life and traction for the work God has set before me. I am truly grateful to have you in my life.

Rich Guerra—You have always fought for me, believed in me, and stood for me. Thank you for always being in my corner.

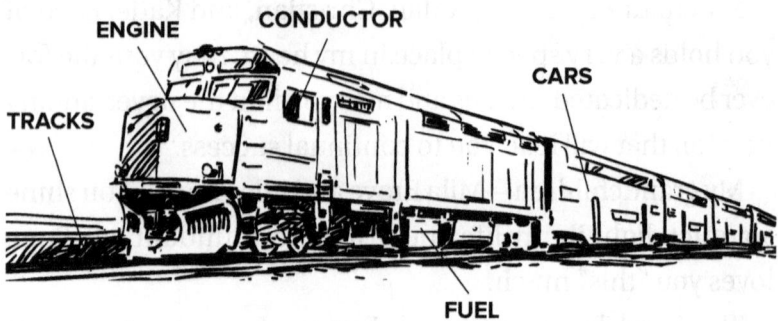

ENGINE

CONDUCTOR

CARS

TRACKS

FUEL

GET ON BOARD

P hil is the pastor of a medium-sized church in the Midwest. Our paths crossed several times over the years, and in each encounter, he always enthusiastically told me that his church was "better than ever," and he was "doing great." More than once, he said, "All good, Chris. The church is growing. God is doing amazing things. I can't imagine anything better. Up and to the right!"

After a few of these assurances, I thought, *This guy is really killing it . . . or he's just using "conference-talk."*

One day, he called me and asked to connect on a Zoom call. I quickly learned the truth behind the glowing reports. He jumped right in: "Chris, I haven't been completely honest with you. I've been the pastor here for eight years. The first two were the honeymoon phase, and things were really good." Tears came to his eyes, and his voice quavered. "That time is long over. For the past six years, I've really struggled. I've tried everything I've heard at conferences—outreach, serving in the community, leadership development, discipleship, software, website, follow-up—the whole thing. Some of them have been successful, but there are two big problems: Our church is stuck, and I feel empty. I don't know what to do." After a pause, he told me, "I don't know how much longer I can keep doing this."

I had enough tact to avoid saying what I was thinking at the time, but after we spent a lot of time together, it was safe for me to tell him, "Phil, you could have asked for help at any time during the last six years . . . but you were too proud to ask for it. I'm really glad you finally made the call." I asked him if he'd like me to tack a day onto one of my trips in his part of the country, so we could spend the day together. He jumped at it. Six weeks later, I walked into his office. We talked for a while, and then I said, "I'd like to spend a little time with the people on your team. If it's okay with you and them, I want to pop in and talk with each one for a few minutes."

He said, "Sure, we'll get back together for lunch."

I walked through the offices and knocked on doors. They all knew I was there for the day, but they didn't think they'd have any time with me. I asked if we could talk for just a little bit, and each one gave me thirty to forty-five minutes. I spent the first minutes just getting to know each one's story, and then I asked for some perspective: "Tell me what it's like being on this team."

A couple of them were obviously hesitant to be transparent with me, but several were bold enough to describe Phil using terms like passive-aggressive, negative, pessimistic, and nit-picking. One of them told me, "He keeps track of every negative thing that happens—and I mean everything! There's no affirmation, no celebration, no encouragement." Another one told me, "Pastor Phil doesn't slow down long enough to know any of us. He's always in a hurry. If anything goes wrong—in other words, it doesn't meet his standard of perfection—he makes sure to point out who's to blame." One of the older and wiser people on the team told me, "I feel really sorry for Pastor Phil. He's always pushing himself. He's so critical, of himself and everyone else, and he never finds anything to feel good about."

Phil wasn't leading in vision and strategy; he was leading in discouragement and fault-finding. He was completely absorbed in every detail that didn't go exactly like he hoped. Most pastors put a positive spin on negative data, but Phil put a negative spin on positive data.

It didn't take a PhD in psychology to realize that Phil's identity was completely tied up in his performance, or more accurately, his lack of perfect performance. He saw himself as defective, a failure, someone who was always coming up short no matter how hard he tried. In those first months I worked with him, I discovered that his wife and children felt emotionally abandoned. He worked eighty to ninety hours a week, and when he was at home, he was either too exhausted or too preoccupied with the church to be genuinely present with them.

The problem wasn't the staff, and it wasn't the strategies and programs they were implementing. The problem was Phil's insecurity. I found a good counselor in his area and connected them. I sent Phil some great books on discovering your identity as a child of God and who we are in him. He went to the counselor, and he read the books, but nothing could dent the iron defenses around his heart. Three months later, he was just as driven, just as self-condemning, and just as miserable as he had been the first day I spent with him. The needle hadn't moved an inch.

I shared a concept with him called "the identity thermostat." Our identity in Christ as a loved, forgiven, accepted, adopted, treasured child of God sets our spiritual thermostat at seventy degrees, and it doesn't matter if the weather outside is twenty below or a hundred degrees. The identity thermostat keeps us comfortable and secure. I then told him, "Phil, I've sent you to a counselor, and I've given you some wonderful books. Your wife is trying to encourage you, and your team is behind you, but none of this is giving you confidence and peace because your identity thermostat is broken. If you don't get it fixed, here's what's going to happen: you're going to lose your best staff members, you'll lose your most faithful leaders in the church, you'll lose your physical health as the unrelenting stress changes your body chemistry, and you'll lose your emotional connection with your wife and kids. You're headed in that direction now, and if you don't change, a crash is coming. I'm sure of it because I've seen it too many times. Soldiers don't follow discouraged generals. They follow leaders who are eager, positive, and hopeful. Phil, things have got to change."

THERE'S AN OLD SAYING, "PEOPLE DON'T CHANGE WHEN THEY SEE THE LIGHT; THEY CHANGE WHEN THEY FEEL THE HEAT."

This wasn't an idle threat—all of these consequences were already in motion, and if he didn't do something soon, they'd become a painful reality. There's an old saying, "People don't change when they see the light; they change when they feel the heat." The threat of these painful consequences finally got to Phil's heart. He became more attentive to his counselor, and he read the books I'd recommended for spiritual refreshment, not just intellectual stimulation. Gradually, his heart began to change. The love of God slowly eroded the granite blocks of perfectionism and self-condemnation.

I gave him some simple and practical steps to take with his team. I told him to build celebrations into the agenda each week in their staff meetings, so people could share what God had done (and what went right), and together, they could be thankful. At first, it was forced (and probably pretty awkward), but soon, Phil and the team created a better culture of optimism and appreciation. He needed to heal all the strained and broken relationships in his life, and he took steps to apologize, listen, and understand.

It wasn't a sudden "Damascus Road" experience for Phil. The real transformation began after about five months of working with him. We focused mostly on his identity thermostat for the next six months, and as he progressed, we began to address other issues in his mission, vision, and strategy. A year after I met with Phil and his team for the first time, the team was functioning better, the mood was more positive, and the church had grown from three hundred to about four hundred.

MY HEART FOR PASTORS

I love coaching pastors. I want to be a pastor's biggest cheer-leader. They're in this role because God has called them, and they have a heart for people: for the lost to come to Christ and the saved to become disciple-making disciples. It may sound like a cliché, but I truly believe that Christ's church is the hope for the world. For the sake of mankind, we've got to keep the lighthouses burning brightly.

Lifeway Research has found that six in ten Protestant churches are plateaued or declining, and more than half saw fewer than ten people become believers in the past year.[1] More than six in ten pastors say that accumulated stress is a burden for them, and almost half point to discouragement and distractions that rob them of joy in leading.[2] I've been a pastor, I am a pastor, and I plan to remain a pastor, so I know what it feels like to be under the gun as a leader of a staff-led, volunteer-driven organization. I've seen success, and I've known failure. I've witnessed the amazing work of God, and I've wondered why He was hiding. I seldom talk with a pastor about a problem I haven't faced.

When the pastor's cell phone rings, the vast majority of people who call want one of three Cs: they want to complain, they need cash, or they want counseling. They're not calling to tell you how wonderful you are! I know the complexity and the pain that comes along with the role, and I know all pastors need someone to champion them. When I send emails

1   Aaron Earls, "How Many Churches Are Actually Growing?" *Lifeway Research*, 5 Feb. 2022, https://research.lifeway.com/2019/03/06/how-many-us-churches-are-actually-growing/.
2   Marissa Postell Sullivan, "Stress Tops Mental Challenges Pastors Face," *Lifeway Research*, 26 Apr. 2022, https://research.lifeway.com/2022/04/26/stress-tops-mental-challenges-pastors-face/

to a group of pastors, I often sign off: *Always in your corner!* —because I am. I fight for pastors and their churches. The kingdom of God is too important to let things slide.

WHEN THE PASTOR'S CELL PHONE RINGS, THE VAST MAJORITY OF PEOPLE WHO CALL WANT ONE OF THREE CS: THEY WANT TO COMPLAIN, THEY NEED CASH, OR THEY WANT COUNSELING.

Right now, we have thirty coaches in our network who work with groups of eight to ten pastors each month. Not long ago, a pastor being coached by one of our people sent me a text and asked if I could spare five minutes to talk to him. I was glad to. When we got on the phone, he began, "Chris, I won't take much of your time. I just want to tell you that no one has ever believed in me like you guys do. It means the world to me." That's why I do what I do. That's what gets me up in the morning. That's what drives me to find more ways to help pastors thrive.

For the first time in America's history, the church is on the decline. The factors are many and varied, but the result is that fewer people claim to be Christians, more churches are closing their doors, and more lost people remain lost. I have a God-given calling, a solemn responsibility, to do all I can do to help pastors and their churches turn the tide and begin growing and thriving once again. Someday, I'll stand before God to give an account of all the resources He has entrusted to me. On that day, I want to be able to say, "I gave it everything I had."

THE TRAIN

Several members of our Church Boom team met to talk about the next steps in our strategy to provide resources for pastors, and as we talked, some vehicle metaphors bubbled up. One guy talked about steering a church like steering a car, another described the way airline pilots make thousands of minor adjustments to stay close to their flight path, and someone else said it's important for churches to stay on track. When we realized we were using those concepts, we decided to see if one could be a controlling metaphor for our consulting work. Finally, we decided to use a train. We noticed that all of the tools, techniques, and resources we provide fit into five components of a train:

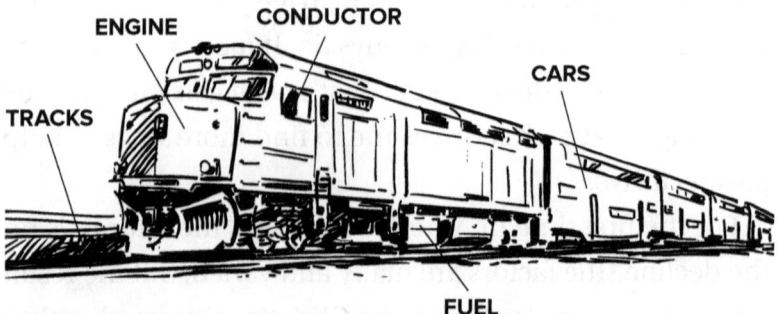

Engine: Growth Strategies

I've worked with pastors of churches that have been at two hundred since the day after Christ's ascension. What can pastors do to create a bump in attendance? In the chapter on growth strategies, we'll address follow-up of visitors, getting people involved more quickly, and streamlining strategies to create more momentum.

Fuel: Leadership and Finances

Everything depends on these resources. Many times, pastors have managers in leadership roles, and that bogs things down. They also may not have an effective leadership ladder to identify potential leaders and grow them into dynamic leaders. I've never talked to a pastor who didn't need more money to accomplish more in the ministry. We'll look at ways to motivate people to give more generously and more cheerfully.

Tracks: Staying on Course

Pastors need to clarify the mission, vision, and values of the church and the team. This isn't a mundane exercise. These concepts are essential for effective strategic planning and regular evaluation.

Conductor: The Essential Role of the Pastor

The pastor's role is crucial. The health, essential skills, and focus of the pastor must be clear and strong. The pastor needs to embrace the responsibilities of the position in a way that feeds his soul instead of depleting it. In this way, he can provide visionary leadership, shepherding, and guidance. As a church grows, the focus of the pastor changes. When the church is at two hundred, he doesn't have the same circle of familiar connections as he did when it was at one hundred. How does he spend his time? Where does he invest his energy? The benchmarks of five hundred, one thousand, and more require continued adjustments, so the pastor has the greatest influence on those who are making the biggest impact. At each level, the decision-making process is different, the criticisms are different, and the stresses are different.

Cars: Alignment of Staff, Leaders, and the Congregation

Effective communication, team-building, and a shared vision create an environment of cooperation and collaboration. It only takes one car to derail many more cars on a train. Pastors need the board, staff team, volunteers, and the entire congregation to function as one. Letting Achan and Absalom spread their poison isn't acceptable for leaders. They need to wade into the controversies, handle conflict, and seek genuine resolution and reconciliation wherever possible.

All of these are designed to give pastors enough traction to move forward. Traction means "to begin to have success,"[3] the kind of power used for pulling or drawing,"[4] and "progress and momentum."[5] In every instance, pastors can use the

---

3   "What Does It Mean to 'Gain Traction'?" *Plain English*, 31 Jan. 2019, plainenglish.com/expressions/gain-traction/.
4   "Traction," *Your Dictionary*, https://www.yourdictionary.com/traction.
5   "Business Traction: What It Is and How to Get It?" *Coresignal*, 15 Feb. 2022, coresignal.com/blog/business-traction/.

principles and exercises in these chapters to get unstuck, so they can move ahead with power and confidence.

In this book, you'll find case studies of pastors and their churches, as well as specific exercises for each part of the train. The exercises are my toolkit as I consult with pastors, and they can now be part of your toolkit. I'm including exercises associated with the topics where I use them most often, but I often mix and match the ones I use with pastors and their teams. Feel free to use any of them at any time. (For quick reference, you'll find a complete list of them in the appendix.)

The metaphor of a train is especially helpful for pastors who feel stuck. A mighty engine with loaded cars is stopped cold before it begins by a seemingly small concrete block on the tracks, but when the same train has momentum, it smashes through the barriers like they are feathers and Styrofoam! My goal is to help pastors get their teams and their churches up to sixty miles an hour, so they can blast through every barrier they face.

When you're stuck, every negative comment is like a knife through the heart, every failure is a catastrophe, and every person who leaves the church is a public indictment (and negative judgment) of your leadership flaws. But if you have momentum, snarky comments don't bother you, failure is a stepping stone of growth, and there are so many people coming that those who leave aren't a threat in any way.

Momentum works for churches of any size. One of our coaches met with a pastor who had about sixty-five people. He told the coach that he was frustrated because they hadn't grown. In addition, he was having a struggle with one of his key volunteers—and he couldn't afford to lose anybody! The coach shared a few principles and strategies, and in only six months, the attendance was holding strong at 130. He had been frustrated and discouraged before, but now he had the swagger of T. D. Jakes! The pastor's relationship with the key volunteer changed because the pastor was no longer afraid to lose him. He could be more direct and give the volunteer clear choices. He told the coach, "He can decide if he wants to stay with us or not." That's confidence. That's momentum!

Some trains have a second engine that pushes the train from the rear of the line of cars. Few people even notice it. That's who I am, and that's who our coaches are. We're behind the scenes, providing strength to move the train of the pastors we coach, so they can move down the tracks with more traction, speed, and momentum. We're not the first engine; we're the second engine helping pastors reach their full potential.

The saying is sure: "Momentum hides a multitude of sins"—not personal sins, but organizational deficiencies. John Maxwell has said many times:

> *Momentum is a leader's best friend because many times it's the only thing that makes the difference between losing and winning. When you have no momentum, even the simplest tasks seem impossible. . . . On the other hand, when you have momentum on your side, the future looks bright, obstacles appear small, and troubles seem inconsequential.*[6]

He's exactly right.

---

6 John C. Maxwell, *21 Irrefutable Laws of Leadership* (New York, NY: HarperCollins, 2002) 163f.

THE SAYING IS SURE: "MOMENTUM HIDES A MULTITUDE OF SINS"— NOT PERSONAL SINS, BUT ORGANIZATIONAL DEFICIENCIES. . . . MY HOPE IS THAT GOD WILL USE THE CONCEPTS IN THIS BOOK TO CLEAR AWAY DEBRIS FROM YOUR TRACKS, SO YOU CAN GAIN TREMENDOUS MOMENTUM.

My hope is that God will use the concepts in this book to clear away debris from your tracks, so you can gain tremendous momentum. When this happens, the things that kept you stuck won't be big problems any longer. They'll only be bumps along the way, and you'll roar past them on the way to fulfill your God-given calling. Nothing less than that.

At the end of each chapter, you'll find some diagnostic questions. Don't rush through these. You don't get extra points for speed! Reflect on them, and use them with your team to stimulate rich conversations about the past, the present, and a bigger and better future.

THINK ABOUT IT:

Virtually all of us have felt stuck at times. When has that been true for you? What do you think was (or is) the root problem?

TRACTION

In the last year, how have you tried to get momentum? What worked? What didn't work?

As you read the brief descriptions of the train metaphor's components, which one(s) do you need to work on? What difference will it make?

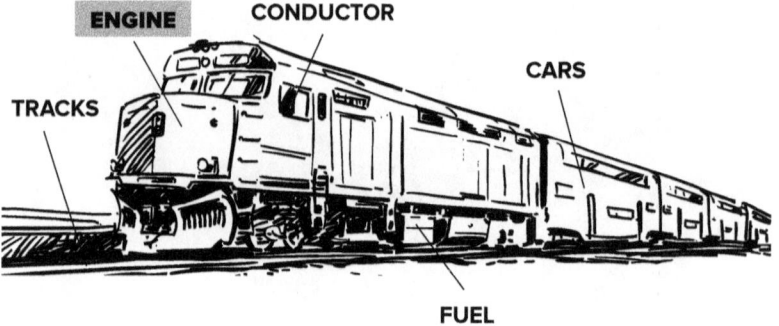

ENGINE

CONDUCTOR

CARS

TRACKS

FUEL

CHAPTER 2

ENGINE: GROWTH STRATEGIES

W hen I met Scott and Angel, they pastored a church of about four hundred in Denver. They asked to meet with me for a couple of reasons: they felt threatened by two people on their team who were creating a rebel congregation within the church, and they were disappointed that they couldn't seem to grow beyond four hundred.

Angel commented sadly, "I thought we could do better than this."

In many ways, the church was in very good shape: they had good cash reserves, their building was at a major intersection, and they had a good reputation in the city. But Scott and Angel's time and energy were being consumed trying to put out fires started by the two defiant staff members.

For obvious reasons, we first tackled the staff problem because it was destroying the cohesion of the team and poisoning the attitude of the volunteers who reported to the two antagonists. I met with the two staff members separately, and when I finished, I walked into Scott's office and told him bluntly, "You need to fire both of them. They're not with you, and they didn't express any desire to get on board with you. They don't like you, and they don't respect you. It's an irredeemable situation. The best thing you can do is fire them as soon as possible and craft your communication to the team and the church to minimize the damage."

Angel looked surprised and said, "I didn't think it would come to that!"

Scott shook his head. He wondered out loud, "What will this say to the rest of our team . . . and the board . . . and the church?"

It took a little while for the idea of terminating them to sink in. I took that as a good sign: Scott and Angel were wrestling with all the implications of this very hard decision. I can count on one hand (and not use three fingers) to signal the number of times I've done something like that. I've counseled plenty of pastors about resolving conflict with team members, but I've suggested immediate termination on only two occasions. Over the next couple of hours, Scott, Angel, and I worked on the staff members' exit strategies.

Scott's questions came like bullets from a machine gun: "What about severance? What about the people who are loyal to them? How do we break the news to the church? What does a transition look like in their areas of responsibility?"

Angel jumped in, "And their families! How will this affect them?"

They asked these and a dozen other very good questions. Finally, we settled on a plan, one they implemented the next day.

Scott called each of them to meet with him in his office. He told them his decision, explained his reasons, and offered a generous severance. Both of them pushed back pretty hard, but Scott remained firm. He asked them to pack up their offices, and he escorted them out of the building. Scott and Angel then met with the team to let them know what was happening, and that Sunday, Scott told the church, "I have some hard news to share with you today." The people in the congregation were divided into different groups: many had no idea about the ongoing resistance, so they were surprised; others were fiercely loyal to the two who had been let go, and they were upset at Scott and Angel. However, those who knew what had been going on far too long were relieved, and they respected Scott and Angel for their courageous decision.

The decision to terminate was the best course for everyone involved, including the two who left that day. At least one has a happy ending. One of them moved to another state, planted a church, found a good coach, and is doing very well. And Scott and Angel have finally built a loving, supportive, cohesive team. They needed someone—and it happened to be me—to step into their lives, give them an honest appraisal of their situation with the two people, encourage them to take the hard step to fire them, and help them communicate wisely to everyone affected, so they could begin to rebuild their team. One of the main reasons their church wasn't growing was that they were investing a lot of time, emotion, and energy into people who, by their own admission, didn't belong there.

The concrete blocks on the tracks were removed that day, and the church began to gain momentum.

In my conversations with Scott and Angel over the next months, we moved on to the second set of issues: growth strategies. As I spent time with them and asked a number of questions, we realized they weren't attracting very many people from their community. They had only about eight guests each week, which was only two percent of those in attendance. They needed to create an "invite culture," so more of their people would actively bring friends and neighbors to church. We also realized that their guests weren't getting engaged—most of them drifted away pretty quickly.

CHURCHES GROW WHEN THEY DEVELOP AN "INVITE CULTURE" TO HELP GUESTS TAKE THE NEXT STEPS OF INVOLVEMENT INTO GROUPS AND SERVING.

The church offered Growth Track, a curriculum to help newcomers get connected, but scheduling was sporadic, and they only had a handful of people each time. Many of those who came out of Growth Track didn't get incorporated into small groups or serving opportunities. The problem was crystalized by this fact: no one on the team owned the strategy to invite and engage guests. Churches grow when they develop an "invite culture" to help guests take the next steps of involvement into groups and serving. Scott and Angel had a system, but it was on life support. I introduced them to a few exercises that would help them create this culture and become much more sticky. (We'll return to their story later in the chapter.)

WORKABLE AND EFFECTIVE STRATEGIES

Every pastor would love to see a numerical bump. They want to reach more people with the gospel, disciple more believers, and build more multiplying leaders. They need strategies that give them traction. The engine represents the driving force behind the ministry's growth. In this chapter, we'll explore and develop effective growth strategies to expand a church's reach and impact. Through a systematic approach to ministry development, pastors will identify opportunities for outreach, community engagement, and discipleship, propelling their church forward.

In my years of consulting with pastors, I'd put them in two camps: the spontaneous and the planners. Those who are from charismatic or Pentecostal backgrounds sometimes look at me like I'm off base when I talk about growth strategies. A few of them are bold enough to speak up and say, "But Chris, we trust in the Holy Spirit."

I always respond, "So do I! I trust Him to give us the wisdom to plan well, so we can be at our best for Christ and His kingdom."

On the other end of the stick, others are so enamored with strategies and techniques they learn at conferences and in books that they rely on these things to cause their churches to grow. But the Spirit and strategies not only *can* coexist, they *must* coexist. I explain it this way: We need to focus on the *hustle*, and God is responsible for the *harvest*. We do our part under the leadership of the Holy Spirit, and God produces the fruit. Our anxiety skyrockets when we feel responsible for producing what only God can produce.

The hustle is, in my opinion, thinking through how we can trust God to maximize our resources by using the most effective strategies to reach more people and build multiplying disciples. How do we connect with the community? How do we motivate the crowd that shows up at our services? And how do we instill vision, passion, and skills into our core leaders? Community, crowd, and core—that's the framework for our growth strategies.

I've talked with many pastors who, for various reasons, arrive at church on Sunday mornings and wonder who will show up. Maybe strategic planning hasn't been modeled for them, maybe they see this kind of planning as sub-spiritual or worldly, or maybe they're so burdened by the stress of the job that they can't muster the energy to devote to planning. Whatever the reason, they miss out on opportunities to grow their church and have a greater impact for the kingdom. The number of those attending on Sunday is the result of your growth strategies (or lack of them) Monday through Saturday.

At Disneyland, the executives created systems to move people forward as efficiently as possible. They don't want any clogs in the process that would frustrate their customers and eventually reduce the number of people who are willing to put up with the hassles.

When I speak at conferences, I may have five hundred people in the room, but I invite audience participation. I ask, "What's your church's mission statement?"

A number of people yell, "To love Christ and fulfill the Great Commission," and variations of that theme.

"Great," I tell them. "How are you going to accomplish your mission? Give me your three most important steps."

I often get blank stares. If you can't adequately answer the *how* question, you're not going to accomplish your *what*, no matter how carefully you've crafted it. I explain, "Let me make it very simple: How do you get people from the community to show up? How do you motivate those who attend, the crowd, to take their next steps of faith (or their first step)? And how do you enlist people to become leaders who lead leaders—those who are the core of your church's strength? The answer to these questions is the bedrock of your strategy."

A lot of pastors feel stuck, and out of desperation, they adopt any strategy that promises to get them off dead center. They hear how this pastor was marvelously successful in this strategy and how another church grew spectacularly by using that strategy. There's nothing wrong with learning from others, and there's nothing wrong with adopting their methods, but too often, pastors don't see the same level of success as the presenters, so they give up too soon. My mentor has told me more times than I can count: "Pick it and stick it!" In other words, choose a strategy you think will work, and work it to get the bugs out (and there are always bugs) until it works for you.

When I talk to a staff team about selecting a good strategy, I ask, "Which exercise machine helps you get in shape better: an elliptical, a treadmill, or a rowing machine?"

They look at me like I'm asking a trick question, and I am. They sometimes argue with each other about which one is better, but after a while, they shrug and say, "It really doesn't matter."

"Precisely," I respond. "Just pick one and stick with it. Find a strategy or two that promises progress, use it, and drive it until the wheels fall off." Or maybe a better metaphor is this: drive it until it has served its purpose, and then fine-tune it, or find something else. I tell people, "If you're pushing a rock up a hill and you decide to take a break or you conclude that it's too much trouble, the rock won't stay where you left it. The natural law of gravity will cause it to roll downhill." When we stop using a strategy, we can expect things to roll back downhill.

I talk to pastors who launched a new initiative with a lot of enthusiasm, but six months later, "stuff" has happened, and they're not giving energy to the program. They often say things like, "My grandmother died, and I had to take care of her estate," "My child got sick," "We bought a new house, and it was a fixer-upper," "I had to spend the last few months trying to work things out with a couple of staff members," etc.

I tell them, "I understand. Things like that happen, but you realize, don't you, that your rock is at the bottom of the hill again, and you have to restart the process of pushing it up the hill?"

When I work with pastors on each of the components of the train, I take them through a process from initial analysis to successful completion.

WHEN I WORK WITH PASTORS ON EACH OF THE COMPONENTS OF THE TRAIN, I TAKE THEM THROUGH A PROCESS FROM INITIAL ANALYSIS TO SUCCESSFUL COMPLETION.

Evaluation

I *evaluate* what's going on. I ask diagnostic questions to find out what's working and what's not, what's the capacity of the pastor and the team, and their history of using growth strategies. We look at the "invite culture" to see how they're reaching into the community. We examine how they follow up with guests. We explore how effectively they move people into Growth Track, small groups, and volunteer opportunities. And we take a look at their leadership pipeline. The number that's a solid benchmark of effective outreach is the number of first-time guests in proportion to total attendance. If they have fewer than five guests per one hundred in attendance, they're not attracting enough people, and they won't keep up with attrition. Other churches attract people from the community, but they're not sticky—they come a time or two, but they don't really connect with anyone or take the next step of involvement.

Education

I *educate* the pastor and the team to explain specific exercises that I believe will help them. The evaluation has identified the strengths and needs, and now we focus on strategies to meet those needs, from community to crowd and from crowd to core. (We'll look at several in each chapter.)

Establishment

Together, we *establish* a plan to implement the new or refined strategy. Quite often, this means the pastor and the team or key volunteers need to adjust how they spend their time and other resources. The *plan* focuses on *priorities* that surfaced in the evaluation and the *people* who are best equipped to follow through. A dream, the *what*, can't be fulfilled without the *how* and the *who*.

Execution

The pastor and the team then *execute* the plan, giving me regular updates so I can encourage them and keep them focused.

Evaluate, educate, establish, and execute—that's how I work with pastors and their teams.

BACK TO PASTOR SCOTT AND ANGEL

We implemented five exercises:

1] The 90-Day Run

This exercise is designed for the staff team. I explained what not to do before talking about what to do. I told Scott and Angel, "If you walk into your next staff meeting and announce: 'I have a vision that we'll go from 400 to 550 in the next year,' how do you think they'll respond?"

Angel said, "Well, I get your point. They don't have a strategy to get there."

"Exactly," I responded. "Now, let's give them a very clear strategy. Let's set goals of *engagement* instead of *attendance*. Let's set a goal to recruit forty new volunteers in the next ninety days. You have eight staff members, so each person's goal is to have five new volunteers at the end of that time. We'll find ways to connect with people to bring them along, and we'll find places where they can serve—not just to have a name on an organizational chart, but to put people in places where they make a difference in the name of Jesus." I let that sink in for a minute, and I could tell Scott and Angel were getting the picture. Then I explained, "Each week in staff meetings, one of the items on the agenda is a report from each person about how they're progressing toward this goal."

Scott said, "Okay, I get it. To get more people to volunteer, we need to attract more and engage more in the first weeks they attend. We need to make those a vital part of our strategy."

"Again, exactly. Higher attendance is the result of greater engagement, not the other way around." I used another metaphor: "Angel, I don't know about women, but when men walk into the gym, they make sure to walk past a mirror to take a good look at their sleek, toned body. But that's the *result* of their workouts, not the *cause*."

She laughed. "And you think women don't look in the mirror? I get it, Chris. You want us to focus on the cause, not the effect."

Scott and Angel presented the 90-Day Run to the team, and they realized they needed to make some serious changes in the way they attract people and retain them. They were now focused on the very achievable goal of enlisting five new volunteers each. They gave reports each week in staff meetings, and at the end of the ninety days, there were forty-two new volunteers. They called me on Zoom, so we could celebrate together.

Scott told them, "Let's do it again!" At the end of the next ninety days, they had thirty-nine new volunteers. Scott saw no reason to change horses, so they did a third 90-Day Run. This time, they had forty-three, and the next time, they had fifty. So, in a year, they had an astounding 174 new volunteers! Within the following year, with all of these eager, dedicated people serving together, the church doubled to eight hundred. They're still doing the 90-Day Run. No need to change something that's working so well.

2] The 90-Day Window

This is a strategy to make the transition of new volunteers smooth and positive. (This fits perfectly with the 90-Day Run.)

I asked Scott and Angel, "What's it like when someone signs up to volunteer?"

Both of them looked confused. Angel asked, "What do you mean?"

"I mean, what happens to someone who says 'yes' to the invitation to volunteer in some area of your church?"

Scott spoke up, "Well, we give that person's name to whoever is head of that area, you know, children, greeters, coffee, and all the rest."

"And how many of them fall through the cracks?"

"Good question," Scott said.

"What if, when they sign up on Sunday, they get a Dream Team Welcome Packet delivered to their home? 'Welcome to the team. We're so glad you're joining us!' Along with a t-shirt, a coffee mug, and anything else that identifies them with the church. What impression would that give?"

The lights were coming on, so I kept going. "Think about it: What is it like for each new volunteer on Day 1, Day 30, Day 60, and Day 90?"

Angel jumped in: "We could give them a Welcome Packet on Day 1, a Swag Bag on Day 30, a personal call from Scott or me on Day 60 to thank them for serving, and a gift card on Day 90!"

"That's it!" I beamed. "Give them the Disney experience. Make them feel like they matter to you more than the stars in the sky. Most of them have been part of other churches, and you want them to tell their friends, 'This church isn't like any I've ever attended. It's wonderful!'"

Megachurches are anomalies. They're the product of God's sovereignty and stellar leadership. The rest of us can grow to our potential if we follow strategies to engage people and invite them to be volunteers, and we make their experience something they'll never forget. That's a choice every pastor can make.

At the end of the 90-Day Window, you've created raving fans, and they'll tell everyone they know about your church.

3] Boxes and Batons

As you see in the graphic, this exercise for the staff team (and perhaps key volunteers) has three boxes side by side. Each one contains related strategies:

- In the first box, you'll find the "invite culture," the Sunday experience, the Welcome Center, and the Next Steps or Growth Track class.
- The second box contains two strategies: serving and small groups.
- The third box contains leadership development and spiritual experiences.

Like relay runners who pass the baton to the next runner, we have batons within each box as well as between each box.

What are the batons that help people move from one to the other? Thanks for asking.

I encourage pastors to find the right person, staff, or key volunteer, to be the champion of each box. Their responsibility is to make each component as powerfully positive as possible, and by the last item in each box, to pass people to the next box using a baton of further engagement. This is what I mean.In the first box, the baton is passed from the first to the next to the next to the next. Each handoff is crucial to maintain engagement and promote deeper involvement. The champion is responsible for making these handoffs happen very smoothly. For instance, the point of the Welcome Center is to funnel people to the Next Steps class. If they don't pass this baton, people may not even know about the class.

The batons between boxes 1 and 2 might be coffee with the pastor, pizza with the pastor, or Growth Track. The goal is to get people in Next Steps engaged in the elements of box 2: serving and small groups. Churches that do it well get 70 to 80 percent of the people making the connections from box 1 to box 2. In other words, if there are fifteen people engaged in Box 1, you can have eleven or twelve serving and/or in small groups very soon.

One of the tragic images in an Olympic relay is when athletes who have devoted their lives to training for the event drop the baton and are disqualified. The first two runners can make a perfect handoff, but if runner number three can't make the connection with the one running the anchor lap, the race is over for all four of them. That can happen very easily in churches: A dozen people sign up on Sunday to serve or join a group, and the names are given to someone in charge, but no call is made. The next Sunday, these people wonder what their commitment really means, and they assume serving and joining a small group aren't really all that important after all.

The baton between boxes 2 and 3 is very intentional. The pastor and the team notice those who have leadership gifts and are already using them, and they create an onramp for them to have a bigger impact. (I'll address the leadership pipeline much more in the next chapter.)

Boxes and batons help people conceptualize the flow of increased engagement. If we assume these transitions will just happen because we have these meetings and events, we'll wonder why they don't work very well. Educating the team about this concept, assigning a champion for each box, and working hard to pass the batons will result in amazing growth. Count on it. I've seen it too many times to doubt it.

Scott and Angel used this exercise with their team to explain the connection of one event to another, assign a champion, and find the best ways to pass all the batons.

4] Riverbanks

A few years ago, I was rafting down a river that had powerful (and exciting) rapids. When I looked at the riverbanks, I realized that the power of the river is actually in its banks. If you take away the river banks, you no longer have a swift-flowing, powerful river. You just have a pond. Every church, in fact, every organization, needs riverbanks. What are they? They are the factors that keep you focused, including your vision, mission, ethics, values, and the clarity of your focus. Those are your river banks. If and when those banks erode (or are blasted by the dynamite of unresolved conflict), the river of your church loses its power. If you want the momentum of your church to flow quickly and powerfully, keep the riverbanks high.

Scott and Angel had several problems with their banks: they had two toxic staff members, their team wasn't in alignment, and they lacked clarity about their growth strategies. That's why their church resembled a pond instead of a powerful river. As we built the riverbanks—firing two trouble-makers, hiring new team members, and using the exercises in this chapter—their banks became strong, and their river flowed powerfully.

5] Creating an Invite Culture

Culture is always driven by three things: the stories you tell, the heroes you make, and the things you celebrate. To turn three into two, culture is shaped by what you allow and what you promote. These factors relate to every aspect of all three boxes in Boxes and Batons—which is everything in the church.

The front door of the church is about outreach in the community, inviting people to church, and engaging the guests so they feel welcome. This is the way people grab the baton and move to the next place in box 1.

As I mentioned, Scott and Angel had only 2 percent guests most weeks. They soon realized that wasn't good enough. If you have less than 5 percent guests each week, you need to shift the culture. How? By telling stories about the behavior you want to be repeated, making heroes of those who bring people, and celebrating every guest. You might say, "I'm too busy to check out all the people who invite and bring people." I get it. I am too. So find someone to do your sleuthing for you. Have this person listen for accounts of those who have brought neighbors and friends, gather the facts, get permission to share them, and give this information to you. It can be very recent, or it can be someone whose life was turned around by the Lord, and you find out someone invited them a year ago to come and start their faith journey.

Then you can talk about these "inviters" and "bringers" from the front, which goes a long way to recraft your invite culture. Or even better, have someone video an interview with both people: the one who brought and the one who came, and show it on a Sunday morning. When you share stories of changed lives, of baptisms, and of other remarkable decisions, be sure to include the one who brought them. The hero, then, isn't just the person whose life has been changed, but also the one who brought them. If you have a video or a story you tell twice a month, you'll create a powerful invite culture.

As trains went through eras of being drawn by horses, then wood and coal, they became a vital part of the nation's economy, moving cattle from the West to the East Coast, grain from the Midwest all over the country, cotton from the South to the mills in the North, and every other form of goods and commodities to market. But there was a problem: many cities and states had their own ways of calculating time, so crossing boundaries proved to be a major headache for scheduling. The growth of train traffic was the driving force in setting the time zones we know today. In the same way, the engines of church-growth strategies almost certainly will require adjustments, streamlining, and a more efficient organization to get the most out of them. Don't despair when you realize your old systems can't keep up!

GROWTH STRATEGIES ARE THE POWERFUL ENGINE OF YOUR CHURCH. TRUST GOD TO GIVE YOU DIRECTION, AND CHOOSE THE EXERCISES THAT ADDRESS YOUR CHURCH'S NEEDS.

A train with a broken-down engine doesn't make any progress, and one that's barely moving doesn't have the power to climb hills or get past obstacles. Growth strategies are the powerful engine of your church. Trust God to give you direction, and choose the exercises that address your church's needs. Use them to build momentum that can blast through every difficulty!

THINK ABOUT IT:

Where are you on the continuum of trusting God to do it all (on one end), depending on strategies (on the other), or blending the two? What would your staff and board say about you in this regard?

Can you relate to Scott and Angel's situation, either with the rebel staff members or feeling the church is stuck? If so, how?

Describe how each of the exercises in this chapter could help you:

- The 90-Day Run:
- The 90-Day Window:
- Boxes and Batons:
- Riverbanks:
- Creating an Invite Culture:

EVALUATE: Which ones do you need to prioritize?

EDUCATE: How will you explain the concepts to your team and your board?

ESTABLISH: What are the first steps you need to take?

EXECUTE: When and how will you implement it (or them)?

Who needs to buy into your plans to use the exercises? How will you communicate your plans to them?

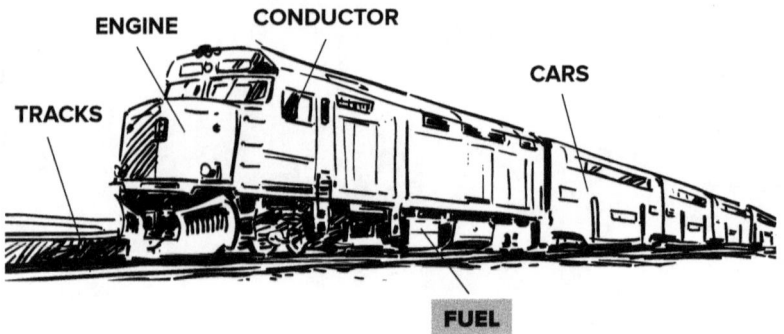

TRACKS

ENGINE

CONDUCTOR

CARS

FUEL

CHAPTER 3

FUEL: LEADERSHIP AND FINANCES

As the delegates to the Continental Congress in Philadelphia were deciding to separate the colonies from the British king, James Watt, a Scottish inventor, came up with the idea of a steam engine. He believed it could be a source of power for all kinds of applications, including the very first iteration of trains, which until that time, were drawn by horses. However, Watt had trouble explaining the concept to investors. To help people grasp the power of his new engine, he used "horsepower" because everyone knew how much a single horse could pull. Horsepower became, and still remains, the unit of measure for power generated in locomotion.

Just as fuel powers a train, a strong leadership pipeline and sound financial management fuel the growth of a church. Pastors need to cultivate a robust leadership development program that identifies, nurtures, and equips emerging leaders within the congregation. Simultaneously, pastors need essential financial management skills to ensure prudent stewardship of church resources and enable sustainable growth.

JUST AS FUEL POWERS A TRAIN, A STRONG LEADERSHIP PIPELINE AND SOUND FINANCIAL MANAGEMENT FUEL THE GROWTH OF A CHURCH.

Without fuel, a train can't run; without the fuel of leadership and money, a church remains stagnant. If you want your church to grow, you can't ignore the fuel.

When I met Carlos and Monica, they pastored a church of about 350 in San Diego. They are Hispanic, their church is in a heavily Hispanic part of the city, and virtually everyone who attends their church is Hispanic. The neighborhood around the church has a high crime rate, and thieves have broken into the church a number of times. Their building has been tagged more times than they can count. To protect the church, they had to erect fences and gates around it. Cultural cohesion was a big plus, but their culture also created some inherent difficulties.

Carlos's father founded the church in the 60s, and Carlos is carrying on the family legacy of spiritual leadership. He is very highly respected. In fact, the culture of *machismo*, valuing masculine pride and power, is the norm in some churches.

I met with Carlos and Monica, along with the executive pastor and his wife, for an hour or so over dinner. When we finished, we met with the team for an exercise I call "Right, Wrong, Missing, Confusing." Everyone gave their input about the state of the church, and it didn't take long to identify two big challenges: leadership and resources. The exercise took a couple of hours. I didn't need that long to uncover the problems, but it was important for everyone on the team to come to the same conclusion. The time was well spent.

Here's what they found: Everyone saw Carlos as the strong man, the *pater familias*, the one who called all the shots. They had people in leadership positions, but they didn't really lead—they were managers with leadership titles. In meetings, there was no expectation of give-and-take in discussing ideas about strategy. When Carlos spoke, it was the end of every discussion. Don't get me wrong: Carlos isn't a narcissist, and he doesn't try to dominate people. He is actually a very kind-hearted, compassionate leader. He was simply acting out the expectations of the culture. Carlos was the boss because everyone fully believed his word was law.

The other major problem at the church was a shaky financial condition. Their cash reserves were meager, and they didn't have enough money to launch new initiatives. As I mentioned, the church is in a disadvantaged part of the city, so there wasn't a pool of wealthy people to write large checks. But on the other hand, very few people in the church were tithing. If they were, the financial strains would be largely resolved.

How would we address the need for high-octane fuel of leadership and finances? Stay tuned.

SIMPLE BUT EFFECTIVE

First, we addressed the issue of finances with several effective exercises.

Follow-Up of First-Time Givers

When people write their first check or make their first transfer, they're making a statement: they find value in your church. At least to some degree, they believe in you enough to part with some of their hard-earned income. Every week, the bookkeeper, accountant, or whoever handles the offering can note the new names on the list of givers and forward that list to the pastor. The pastor then sends a handwritten note that says something like this:

> *Dear _____,*
>
> *Our records show that you gave to our church for the first time last week. (Our records may be wrong, but that's what they told me.) I want to thank you for partnering with us in reaching people and helping them grow in their relationship with God. I appreciate you for believing in us and our mission!*

This brief, personalized note shows appreciation and connects the person to the pastor. It takes a few minutes, but it pays big dividends.

Follow-Up of Splash Giving

A splash gift is something out of the ordinary. A person may regularly give $100 a week but then send a check for $8000. The person may have sold some property, received an inheritance, or gotten a bonus. Whatever the reason, it's special—to the person and to you, the one entrusted with the generous gift.

I recommend one of two approaches: a handwritten note or a phone call. When I make this suggestion, some pastors ask, "Well, what do I say?"

I'd say:Our accountant told me about your generous gift last week. That's incredible! I don't know what happened that enabled you to give so much, but I want you to know that I really appreciate it. We'll use it to reach people with the message of God's love and help them grow in their faith. Thanks for trusting us.

I've found that when I make calls like this, the Lord often uses it to attach their gift to their gratitude for something He has done in their lives, usually recently. For instance, a woman told me, "Pastor Chris, I'm just so thankful God has worked in my daughter's life to bring her back from her addiction. My gift is just a small way to say, 'Thank You!' I got a bonus at work, and I wanted to give it all to the Lord."

Carlos and Monica didn't need a lot of preparation or lead time to implement these two strategies. They started the very next week. All it took was a single call to the church's accountant.

THE 90-DAY CHALLENGE

This exercise took a little more prep time. I explained, "Sometime during the next few months, plan on a sermon series that touches on money at least one week. For instance, you could have a 'Managing Your Life' series. The first week could be on spiritual development, the second on family relationships, the third on managing money wisely, and the fourth on friendships. Or the four-week series could be all about money: budgeting in the first week, comparison and materialism the second week, tithing (or generosity) the third week, and getting out of debt the last week. There are lots of options. The point is that on the third week, you address tithing clearly and attractively.

"As a part of that message, read the passage from Malachi about God challenging us to test him, and then say, 'For the next ninety days, I want all of us to test God with our tithing.' Give everyone a card with a commitment statement, the biblical promise that God will answer, and a place for their names, cell numbers, and email addresses. Ask them to fill them out and turn the cards in that day. In messages for the next ninety days, encourage people to keep their commitment. Send an email or a text the day after the cards are turned in, then again after thirty days, sixty days, and ninety days.

"In sermons, emails, and texts, share passages of scripture, stories of God's provision, and stories of tenacious commitment even when it appears God isn't providing. It's really powerful when you can tell stories about people who encountered setbacks, and then God did something amazing. It's not always a straight-line path when God fulfills His promises."

Carlos planned a four-week series to begin a few months later. When he completed his talk about tithing, ninety people turned in cards. That's a very encouraging number because, of the 350 attending each week, many were couples, and many others attended only occasionally. At the end of the ninety days, fifty were still tithing. Were Carlos and Monica disappointed? Not in the least. That's far more people tithing than they'd ever had before! In these three months, the church's finances were on a more solid footing. It just took a little planning, a clear challenge, regular encouragement, and celebration of God's provision.

Generosity Calendar

As an extension of the 90-Day Challenge, I encouraged Carlos and Monica to think through their year (every year) to plan when they'd have their four-week series that included the 90-Day Challenge. They also put Dave Ramsey's *Financial Peace* on the calendar. It proved to be so helpful that they decided to have it twice a year. We talked about weaving the principles of generosity into their models of discipleship, either in small groups or in classes. This became a clear and comprehensive plan to teach people the importance of generosity—no strong-arming, no guilt, no pressure of any kind, just solid biblical teaching and encouragement to trust God with their money.

Tiers of Giving

In every church, pastors can fairly easily identify levels (or tiers) of giving. This is important, so they can tailor their teaching and encouragement to each level and then help people move up to the next tier. First, break down the tiers of giving into three, and no more than four, categories. For instance, you may have a group that gives $1 to $1,500 per year. The next group might give $1,500 to $5,000, and then $5,000 and up. The key is to find a natural break in the giving, which is pretty easy if you take a good look at the accountant's database.

This information gives you a snapshot of where people are and where they could be if they were encouraged to give more generously. For instance, are they just tipping the pastor for his service? Are they starting to give fairly regularly? Are they consistent tithers? Are they going above and beyond the tithe? (Of course, you can never really know because you don't know their incomes.) Do your best to identify the categories.

With this information, you can host a once-a-year dessert night for each category. They can be held on consecutive weekends. Some pastors host them toward the end of the year, possibly in early November. You can call these "Team Night" or "Celebration of Faithfulness," and let people know they're invited to celebrate their involvement in fulfilling the mission of the church.

The first dessert night can be with people who give $1 to $1,500. You will celebrate them, talk about all God has done, hear a few testimonies, and have a video showing the impact of the church in the community. In the last 15-20 minutes, turn the corner and talk about giving. Thank them for giving, and then challenge them to trust God for a little more. Maybe that would be $25 more per month or to trust him with a tithe. This event gives you the opportunity to share your heart, appreciate people, and challenge them to take the next step in their walks with God. And you're talking to people who are all in (relatively) the same place with their giving. In this way, you can address the unique challenges and opportunities in each tier. At times, we preach on tithing when some of the people are already tithing. But in this case, we know exactly who is in the room. (Of course, you don't call these "tier 1, 2, and 3." Give them all the same generic but encouraging name: Team Night, Celebration of Faithfulness, Serving Celebration, All-In, etc.)

Use the same format for tier 2 at the next dessert night. In this group, a number of people are probably tithing but not all. Those in tier 3 are probably tithing, so you can appreciate them for their faithfulness to God's invitation. If you want to address people who are extraordinarily generous, tier 4, you might have only a dozen people there, and you can have dinner at your house to make it even more special. Celebrate as you did on the other nights, but in the last 15-20 minutes, thank them for their faithfulness and explain that the church is having a greater impact because of their generosity.

The tiers aren't useful only in planning these desserts. The designations enable you to send notes tailored for each one to each group during the year.

In the second year when Carlos and Monica held these celebrations, they found that some who had been in tier 1 the previous year had moved up to tier 2, and some who had been in tier 2 had moved to tier 3. And that year, there were twenty people who had been giving extraordinary amounts and came for dinner at their house.

Gradually, more people were giving, and more were giving more than ever. This strategy provided more resources for the kingdom, and it proved to be an integral part of disciplining people to believe God for more.

I also talked with Carlos and Monica about leadership development. On that first night with the team, we used a simple but effective exercise.

Right, Wrong, Missing, Confusing

This is an exercise with the staff and/or key leaders of the church. On a large whiteboard, write these words at the top of four quadrants: "Right, Wrong, Missing, Confusing." First, ask what's right about the church. This is the easy one. The team often gives feedback like this: no debt, good location, terrific volunteers, friendly people (that always makes it on the board), and other positive things about the church. Write each one on the board.

Then, move to the next category: wrong. Ask the team to voice what they think is wrong about the church. They may be hesitant at first, so you might need to prime the pump by listing one or two. Sooner or later, they'll come up with things like systems don't work well enough, unclear on our follow-up, debt, bad location, not enough money for the programs we want to start, need a better leadership pipeline, etc.

The third part is what's missing. They will probably need help understanding what this means, but stick with it—this is important! They may need help to discover the lack of a good, working, volunteer onboarding process, follow-up of new converts, or the need for a leadership pipeline.

The fourth topic is to identify what's confusing. Again, they may need help from the pastor or coach. Examples might be: vision isn't clear, leaders don't know how to help people take their next steps, team members have overlapping responsibilities, and unsure who we really are as a church.

The first category helps them celebrate what's working well at the church. The other three categories open their eyes to see the challenges. The process takes some time, but in the end, the team "owns" their conclusions about the problems because they're the ones who identified them. People support what they create, so if they create the list, they'll be more likely to get behind the solutions. This means they'll have more commitment to the strategies (and changes in responsibilities) when they work through the problem-solving process.

Leadership Ladder

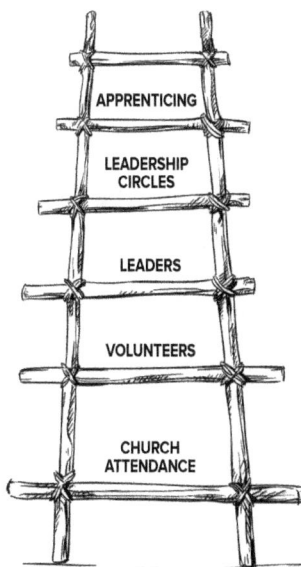

This is a simple tool to help pastors and their teams grasp the flow of leadership development. It's similar to the Tiers of Giving in that it identifies where people are and where they can go next. At the bottom is the entire congregation, the "universe of potential leaders" in the church. Next are the volunteers. These people serve faithfully, but they're not necessarily leaders. (Think of greeters, ushers, people who make coffee, etc.) Next are people in leadership positions: small group leaders, task leaders, and those who lead serving teams. Again, they may not actually be leading, just managing the people who report to them. The next rung up the ladder is leadership circles where leadership development takes place. (I'll describe this in more detail next.) And finally, some pastors identify one or two rising stars and invite them to be apprentices for a season.

LIKE ANY SKILLED CRAFTSMAN, WHEN AS MUCH AS A YEAR IS REQUIRED FOR AN APPRENTICE TO BE CREDENTIALLED, YOU NEED A PATIENT, INTENTIONAL PROCESS TO DEVELOP CHARACTER, WISDOM, AND SKILLS.

Like any skilled craftsman, when as much as a year is required for an apprentice to be credentialled, this is a patient, intentional process to develop character, wisdom, and skills. For six to nine months, take them with you as much as possible, ask good questions, and invite their questions. Let them take a peek behind the curtain to see not only what you do in public but how you prepare in private. For instance, if you see someone who seems primed to take a major role in the children's ministry, that ministry leader can invite the person to be an apprentice for an extended season. Together, they walk through the joys and challenges, and gradually, the existing leader can turn over responsibilities to the apprentice. In the end, the now-skilled new leader can take an important position in that ministry, assume the lead role at a satellite campus, or take over the primary role at the central campus.

Leadership Circles

I love baseball, and I'm always looking for ways to connect the game with leadership principles. The very best Major League teams have outstanding farm teams, especially Triple-A and Double-A. In the farm system, they have great coaches who work with players to develop their talents. Only some of them will make it to the majors, but all of them will improve their ability to play the game. Churches need a farm system to develop leadership talent. I call this strategy "leadership circles."

Twelve years ago, Moses Camacho was one of our ushers. In my brief interactions with him, I could tell he was all-in with Jesus and our church, so I invited him to join me and a small group of people in a six-month study group—a leadership circle.[7] I met with him individually several times over these months, and each time, I came away with a definite sense that God was calling him to some kind of ministry. (At the time, he was a married middle school teacher.) When I made this observation, he shook his head and said, "Chris, that sounds great, but I can't. It would be a huge upheaval for me and my family."

I encouraged him to pray about it, and we continued to meet. A few months later, he joined our team as our small group pastor. He was obviously very gifted, so I promoted him to be our executive pastor. He excelled there too, so I asked him to supervise our eleven campuses. I'm sure Moses was a wonderful schoolteacher, but when I identified his anointing and called him out, he moved heaven and earth to change roles, so he could be what God had designed him to be.

I'm sure there are a hundred ways to create pathways for people who are called to vocational ministry, but one particular strategy, my leadership circles, has been incredibly effective. About every six months, I look for people who demonstrate a measure of passion and talent—people who seem primed for "more," whatever more might be, perhaps as a group leader, an elder, or some pastoral role—and I invite them to meet together with me for the next six months. I pick a leadership book, and we dive in once a month, often

---

7 Chris Sonksen, "The Church as a Farm Team," *Influence*, 17 May 2023, influencemagazine.com/en/Practice/The-Church-as-a-Farm-Team.

covering two chapters at a time. I meet with each one indi-vidually several times during those months—and I listen. I want to hear what God has done and what He's doing. I want to affirm their anointing and help them find the place where they can serve most effectively. Of course, I don't hit grand slams like Moses every time, but there are enough singles, doubles, and triples to let me know these farm teams produce real results.

Out of the handful of people in each leadership circle, I may mentor one or two of them. We continue to meet to explore God's will and equip them for their next steps. Many of them will need (and want) some credentials to prepare them and demonstrate their commitment to excellence. Some may enroll in a Bible college or seminary, and others will find online courses they can complete before or after work each day. A number of denominations have excellent online courses and degrees. Acquiring additional education may not be necessary, but I believe it's enormously helpful because it tests them and confirms their calling.

The strategy of forming leadership circles solves two problems: It answers the question of where future leaders in the *wider church* will come from—they come from the abundant talent called out by each church's farm team. And it answers the question of where *your church's* leaders will come from—they'll come up through your system, not from free agency.

Carlos and Monica started their leadership circles. He gathered a group of men, including some staff members, and she gathered a group of women, also including some who were on the staff team. For six months, they met twice a month with these groups. They studied a leadership book that had twelve chapters, so they covered a chapter in each meeting. They met for an hour. For the first forty minutes, they talked about the content of the chapter. For the rest of the time, Carlos and Monica asked them two questions: "What's the single most important thing you learned from this chapter?" and "What are you going to do about it?" These two questions are crucial.

After Carlos and Monica finished their leadership circles, they asked each of the people who completed their study to start their own leadership circles. So, instead of two circles with about eight each, there were now sixteen circles with about seven each. By the end of the year, 112 people had completed leadership circles—in a church that began this strategy with 350 attending on an average Sunday.

The result wasn't just numbers. They were creating rich leadership conversations, a far stronger leadership culture, a pipeline to grow more leaders, and specific people who were motivated to lead ministries in the church. The farm system also surfaced some people who were interested in vocational ministry, so Carlos and Monica helped them to be prepared to serve on their expanding team or be part of a church plant nearby.

If you want your church to grow, you need more leaders, and you need more resources. If you want to plant a church or start a new campus, you need competent leaders who are already ready to go, and you need plenty of money. If your denomination wants you to take over a struggling church with a leaky roof fifteen miles away that now has only a handful of people, it's not the time to wonder where you can find leaders and money. It's far better to have these rising leaders already available and chomping at the bit to get going and to have cash in the bank to invest in the acquisition. If you send a few warm bodies and a few meager dollars to that situation, there's a high likelihood of it becoming a first-rate disaster. At that point, you've discouraged the people you sent, and you've wasted a lot of money. You can do better than that.

IF YOU WANT YOUR CHURCH TO GROW, YOU NEED MORE LEADERS, AND YOU NEED MORE RESOURCES.

There's another principle related to all this: if you develop a vibrant leadership pipeline and a strong financial footing, just watch to see the doors of opportunity God opens for you. You've proven He can trust you to take advantage of those opportunities. I tell pastors, "If you dig the ditch, God will send the rain." Digging the ditch is the hard work of developing leaders and raising money. If you'll do that, you'll be surprised at what God sends your way.

As Carlos and Monica used these strategies, they saw remarkable results. eighteen

Financially, giving grew by 12 percent within a year and another 21 percent in the second year. For the first time in the history of the church, they had cash reserves, and the money they invested in new programs paid big dividends in lives changed and greater enthusiasm among their people. They developed a leadership culture: many of those who had been managers with leadership titles learned how to lead.

As I met with the team during these months, I noticed their language change—they asked better questions, they had sharper insights, and they connected the dots more quickly between strategy and implementation. More than once, I thought, *Wow, that staff member wouldn't have asked that question eighteen months ago!* The congregation grew because so many new leaders were taking ownership of every part of the ministry, and they decided to start another service on Saturday night. They certainly couldn't have done that before because they didn't have enough leaders. In addition, they were able to add new ministries of outreach in the community and pastoral care, and they became a beacon of hope for those in the community who struggle with debt.

The last time I talked to Carlos, he was considering starting a campus a few miles away in another part of the city. I told him that it wasn't enough to find the right campus pastor; he needed to find the right staff team to launch the new campus.

What do pastors worry about? Money and people. If they had more money and more leaders, they'd sleep better at night. Trains have morphed over the years to use more powerful and efficient fuels, but in churches, the fuel remains the same: it's all about the valuable resources of leaders and money.

TRAINS HAVE MORPHED OVER THE YEARS TO USE MORE POWERFUL AND EFFICIENT FUELS, BUT IN CHURCHES, THE FUEL REMAINS THE SAME: IT'S ALL ABOUT THE VALUABLE RESOURCES OF LEADERS AND MONEY.

THINK ABOUT IT:

Who are some pastors you know who don't have enough leaders or money? What is the impact of that deficit in their lives and ministries?

Who are some pastors who do have enough leaders and money? What's different about them, their teams, and their churches?

Who are some people in your church who are managers with leadership titles? What are you going to do about that?

Who are the rising stars who need more of your attention?

Do you think investing time in leadership circles would be time well spent? Why or why not?

EVALUATE: Which of the exercises related to money look most attractive to you?

EDUCATE: Explain how you would use them and what difference they would make.

ESTABLISH: What are your first steps of implementation?

EXECUTE: When and how will you take those steps?

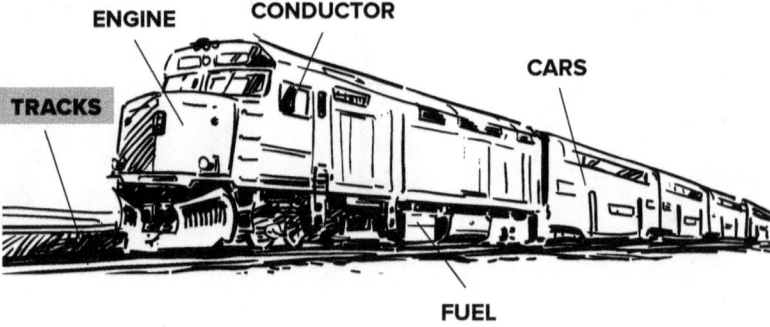

ENGINE CONDUCTOR CARS TRACKS FUEL

CHAPTER 4

TRACKS: STAYING ON COURSE

T racks represent the path that the ministry follows. Pastors and their teams need to navigate a vast array of challenges and opportunities while staying true to the church's vision and mission. Through strategic planning and regular evaluation, they can ensure their ministry stays on course toward its intended destination.

THROUGH STRATEGIC PLANNING AND REGULAR EVALUATION, PASTORS AND THEIR TEAMS CAN ENSURE THEIR MINISTRY STAYS ON COURSE TOWARD ITS INTENDED DESTINATION.

In the earliest years of trains, railroad tracks were made of wood, but when engines were converted to steam power in the early nineteenth century, wooden tracks proved too fragile to support the heavier weight. An English engineer, John Birkinshaw, found a solution: he invented long wrought iron rails nailed with spikes or bolts to the cross timbers.

Today, we sometimes see maintenance crews examining tracks to be sure the rails are secure, and there are no impediments that could derail a train.

Birkenshaw's innovation is a metaphor for today's churches. As our churches grow, we need to give more attention to the strength of our rails: our mission, vision, and values. And we are the maintenance crew, always checking to be sure the rails are secure and clearing the tracks of anything that might cause a disaster.

A LITTLE CONFUSED

I met Vincent and Katrina at a conference, and after they heard me speak, they asked me to fly to New Jersey to meet with them and their team. A few months later, I sat down with them in Vincent's office. He explained that he was a little confused (okay, maybe more than a little). The church grew for the first five years they'd been there, but since then, over the previous seven years, it had plateaued, seldom below 350 and never above four hundred. They had two campuses, but the second one was more of an afterthought when the denomination asked them to take over a dying congregation about fifteen miles away. Their strategies were good ones, and they had some good leaders. They also had a decent amount of money in the bank. After listening to their status report, *I* was confused. With so many pluses, why were they stuck? What roadblocks were preventing their growth?

I traveled to meet with them two more times, and to be honest, I was stumped. Their services were good, they had a lot of small groups, and they reached out into the community in evangelism and serving opportunities. Other pastors would die to have their location at the intersection of two main roads in their community, so they had plenty of visitors. They also had some strong people on their team. A lot was right, so why weren't they thriving? (After many years working with pastors and their teams, I have enough experience to pinpoint problems and find solutions fairly readily, but for a long time, I couldn't put my finger on the issues with this church.)

On my fourth visit, I met with several people on the staff team. When I met with the worship leader, I asked him what makes their church stand out. He thought for a long time, and then he said, "I have no clue."

I asked, "What do you mean?"

He continued, "Oh, I love working with Vincent and Katrina. They're wonderful people." Another pause, and then, "I'm not sure what our edge is . . . what makes us go . . . what makes us stand out. Sure, we could have a little better music, a little better preaching, a few more small groups, and a little better youth and kids programs, but all of those seem to be doing pretty well. Underneath it all, I'm not sure what we're about. I'm not sure where we're going, so I don't know the road to get there."

Finally, someone had identified the issue for me!

Later, when I met with Vincent, I cut through all the talk about strategies and systems. I asked him, "What do you really want at your church?"

He looked a little surprised by my question. He could have answered in any number of ways, but after a few seconds, he made it very personal: "I want to be the lead pastor of a great church."

I responded, "Okay, great. But what differentiates your church from the others in your city? When you and I have gone to lunch, we pass more than a dozen churches. Why would someone come to your church instead of theirs?"

Vincent thought for a while, and then he looked at me and said solemnly, "I have no idea."

This conversation was the key to unlocking the problems and potential of their church. As we continued to talk, both of us realized he wasn't clear about the church's identity, mission, vision, and values. Those are the tracks churches run on, and they're often neglected or taken for granted. Vincent and Katrina needed to replace their wooden rails with some new iron ones. I began a discussion with them about their USP: their *ultimate strategic position.*

I've walked into staff meetings where poison was dripping from each person's lips, so it was easy to identify the problem. That wasn't the case at all at Vincent and Katrina's church. They loved the people on the team, and that love was returned. The culture wasn't toxic, but neither was it intentional. They were just rocking along, doing the same things they'd done for years, and expecting bigger and better results. When those results didn't materialize, they looked at all the good things going on, and they couldn't figure out how to move forward. That's when they asked for my input.

Let me commend Vincent and Katrina. In many respects, they had things really good. Their church was stable, their team got along well, they were being paid adequately, and they lived in a nice part of town. They could have told me, "Hey, Chris, we're good. Nothing to see here. Nothing to change. Good to see you. Goodbye." But they didn't. The Lord had put a holy discontent in their hearts. They wanted to have a bigger impact for Christ and His kingdom, but they didn't know how.

MISSION, VISION, STRATEGY, AND VALUES

Leaders define mission and vision in different ways, but they're almost interchangeable. Here's my shot at them: *Mission* answers the "what" question. *Vision* answers the "where are we going" question. And *strategy and values* answer the "how" question.

MISSION ANSWERS THE "WHAT" QUESTION. VISION ANSWERS THE "WHERE ARE WE GOING" QUESTION.

At South Hills, where I'm the founding pastor, our vision statement says: "We want to connect people to Jesus in every state and on every continent by developing leaders and creating irresistible churches." Our mission statement is: "Leading unchurched people into a growing relationship with Jesus Christ." Everything I am and everything we do at our church are about this what and this where. If you ask people who know me, "Does Chris want to develop leaders and create irresistible churches?" they'd respond, "Are you kidding? He bleeds that stuff!"

When I met with Vincent and Katrina, we began to clarify and articulate their mission: What are you about? What are you trying to accomplish? What makes you different? The vast majority of churches have similar mission statements: "To reach unchurched people and make them fully devoted followers of Christ." When pastors tell me this is their mission, I ask, "So, tell me how you're reaching out in your community to reach unchurched people." If they can't rattle off a bunch of things they're doing to accomplish that purpose, I know they aren't really serious about their mission. They may say the right things, but something else has captured their minds and hearts.

I used a number of exercises with Vincent, Katrina, and their team.

Riverbanks

I've applied this illustration in many settings to make important points. (See the explanation in chapter 2.) Vincent and Katrina needed to understand that narrowing their vision is ultimately more productive than trying to do a little of everything.

Core, Aspirational, and Accidental Values

Quite often, pastors, boards, and teams make grand pronouncements of their values: "We want to fulfill the Great Commission." "We love God with all our hearts and our neighbors as ourselves." "We're generous people, and we use our resources for God's kingdom." "We're reaching the unchurched in our community to make them dedicated disciples of Christ." And on and on. These leaders often tell me, "These are our core values," but they're really not. They're *aspirational*. Our vision statement at South Hills is a good case in point: we're pushing toward those incredibly lofty goals, but unless there's a movement of God like we haven't seen since the Second Great Awakening, we won't get there in my lifetime.

We don't need to put aspirational values on our sign in front of the church; we just need our leaders to understand that we're shooting for the stars.

Core values are about the pastor, the board, the staff team, and the key volunteers at the church. They describe who you are no matter what—when everyone is watching and when no one is watching, when everything is going well, and when you face a crisis.

Years ago, I asked a consultant to come to our church to find out what makes us tick. He met with our staff members, and then he came back to give his report to me. He said, "Chris, one of your core values is reaching the lost. Everybody said that's who you are, and that's what this church is about. They told me that another core value is risk-taking. You're willing to do crazy things to accomplish your goals. The last one that many people mentioned is the tandem of humor and sarcasm."

"Well," I responded, "I expected the first two, but I'm surprised at the third one: humor—okay, I get that. But sarcasm? Really?"

He laughed and told me, "C'mon, Chris. Every time I'm with you and your team, everybody is making good-natured fun of each other. It's who you are—all the time. It may not work on other teams, but it's part of the glue that holds you together."

"Yep," I answered. "You're exactly right, but I don't think I ever would have said it's a core value."

You might think this was just a fun exercise, but it quickly turned more serious. When I told my mentor about the consultant's feedback, he laughed and said, "Bull's-eye!" I tried to push back a little, and then he asked, "Chris, whom was the last person on your team you had to let go?"

That was an easy one. "It was just a couple of months ago. It was a guy who was here for over a year, but he didn't really fit with our culture."

"And why is that?"

"Because he couldn't take a . . ." I stopped before I said the last word.

"Because he couldn't take a joke, right? I'm sure there were other issues related to his performance, but the first thing that came to your mind was that he didn't fit your culture of humor and friendly sarcasm. Chris, that's a core value. Admit it."

But he wasn't finished with me. He asked, "And whose fault is it that he didn't fit?"

I scanned my mental roadmap for an exit ramp, but I couldn't find one. He answered for me, "It's your fault! You hired a guy who didn't represent one of your core values, and then you let him go because he didn't fit well enough."

That was a teachable moment for me. I've told that story countless times because it reveals how easy it is to make assumptions that are costly, not only to you but to everyone else.

The third category is *accidental* values. You didn't intend for them to become an integral part of your culture, but they did. For instance, I talked with the people on the executive team of a large church in the Midwest. I knew their founding pastor had a "no debt" policy from the beginning over forty years before. And, as I met with each person on the team, they all talked about the senior pastor's amazing generosity.

When I probed a bit, though, each one of them had another assessment: "But he absolutely hates conflict, so we find all kinds of ways to avoid having hard conversations. He spiritualizes it to say, 'We just need to forgive and move on,' but hurt feelings and misunderstandings have lingered—on our executive team—for years." Another person on the team explained it this way: "He chooses friendship over leadership." The unwillingness to deal with hard things became an accidental value of the pastor, the team, and the church. Let me put it another way: artificial harmony is an oxymoron because real harmony is never artificial. You have to work at it, especially when it's uncomfortable and it makes you feel vulnerable.

Another accidental value is staff members working long hours to prove their worth to the pastor or the pastor working long hours to prove himself to the board. Hard work is commendable, but wise work is far better than pushing yourself to the point of burnout.

HARD WORK IS COMMENDABLE, BUT WISE WORK IS FAR BETTER THAN PUSHING YOURSELF TO THE POINT OF BURNOUT.

Some people on teams feel insecure, and their coping strategy is to always have the best solution for any problem. Having good ideas isn't a crime, but always finding fault with others' ideas saps a team of creativity and ruins chemistry among people. Again, if it's not addressed, it can become a detrimental accidental value that shapes the attitudes and behavior of every person on the team.

These conversations crystallized Vincent and Katrina's thinking and sharpened their definitions of core, aspirational, and accidental values. They realized coasting had become an accidental value, and careful critiques hadn't been a regular part of their culture. Still, I didn't think we'd hit the sweet spot—not yet, at least.

Right, Wrong, Missing, Confusing

I've already described in chapter 3 how this exercise works, but let me explain how I used it with Vincent and Katrina. After my conversation with the worship leader, who told me he enjoyed his role at the church but didn't know where things were going, I gathered the team together and drew the four quadrants on the whiteboard. I let them start by listing the things that were going right at the church, and then things got more interesting. They didn't have many things they could list under "wrong," but the conversation about "missing" and "confusing" was enlightening—especially to Vincent.

The people on the team loved him and didn't want to hurt his feelings, so they didn't want to create any unnecessary waves by pointing out that they weren't clear about the church's vision. However, I finessed it out of them. This exercise helped Vincent understand that his lack of clarity was contagious. We didn't solve all the problems in that exercise, but it's not designed to. It's effective in surfacing often-neglected issues and prompting long-overdue conversations. It certainly did that.

Your Heart, God's Heart, and Community Needs

The church had a mission statement that was clear and strong. No problem there, but the vision, the "where we're going," wasn't clear at all. I was certain there was more to Vincent than I'd seen, so I planned to ask a few more pointed questions. Before that, I asked several staff members to tell me about any themes that came up often in Vincent's messages.

They all told me his best illustrations are about his traumatic childhood. Instantly, I knew they were onto something.

I met with Vincent when we weren't pressed for time (imagine that!), and I asked him more about his life and his journey of faith. He told me about a very troubled childhood. His father had been an alcoholic, and his mother was a heroin addict. We talked about how growing up in their home affected him, and he told me two things that rang bells for me: the hurt, fear, anger, and shame he experienced for so many years gave him tremendous compassion for broken people—addicts, as well as those affected by them. And his longing to provide resources for people who struggle with substance abuse and their family members. As he spoke, tears filled his eyes.

God's heart is always for the lost and broken, but each pastor has a unique story to bring to the leadership position. All of us have committed sins and suffered wounds, but the effects can be widely varied. The point of this exercise is to uncover the pastor's heart and see how God might use him to care for specific people in the community. A seminary professor tells his students, "The difficulties you experience in your first forty years will become the platform for an abundant ministry for the rest of your life." His point is clear: a pastor's struggles may have been severe, but God will use anything—absolutely anything—for the good of people and for His glory if we'll let Him.

As we talked, the lights came on for Vincent. He said, "I want our church to be known as the people who care about all who are affected by substance abuse."

I replied, "Why don't you invest your heart in that? Why don't you lead your church to become a haven for these people?"

It became evident that Vincent's heart was primarily focused on men, not because he didn't care about women and children, but because men are often the ones who devastate everyone in the home when they're caught up in substance abuse. I suggested he have two points of focus: building men inside the church to be spiritual leaders in their homes and reaching men outside the church with the gospel and resources to help them get off and stay off addictive substances. I asked, "What would it look like to focus on those two things?"

His wheels were turning like I hadn't seen in the months we'd been meeting. Vincent launched into ideas about programs for men in the church and outreaches in the community. He talked nonstop for forty-five minutes while Katrina and I just listened and nodded. I thought, *Okay, Lord. Bingo! This is it!*

Vincent redefined the center of the mission to "be the church that raises up spiritually strong men." He and Katrina started rewriting job descriptions, reworking the organizational chart, and moving resources. They found excellent Bible study resources for men and started classes and groups. They even changed the décor of the church to be more attractive to men: every few weeks, they had a muscle car or a Harley Hog sitting in the church lobby. In the summer, they had big plasma screen televisions outside the front of the church showing games and races on ESPN. Vincent wanted to create a place and an environment where men would tell others, "Hey, you gotta come check this out!" The church started growing—and a lot of the visitors were all tatted up!

Vincent's vision expanded, and he dreamed of having a home for men who were coming out of addiction. The dream found legs when someone on the city council found out about Vincent's plan and offered the church a building nearby that could be renovated to house fifteen men. The council member told Vincent, "As long as you do something that benefits the city, you can have the building." He jumped at it!

I told Vincent like I've told so many pastors: "Dig the ditch, and God will send the rain," and he did. Within six months, the renovations were completed, and the home was opened.

A few months later, someone in our organization connected Vincent with a state agency that provides grants for causes like this. Not long after Vincent applied, he received a check for $250,000 to care for men in the city. Within two years, the church opened another rehab home and planted another campus in the city, and the main campus grew to about seven hundred people on an average Sunday. Vincent had been transformed from a confused and struggling pastor who lacked clarity about his focus to a man with a God-given mission, God-given resources, and results that can be traced back to God-ordained conversations.

I tell pastors that they need a dream that will capture the hearts of everybody in the congregation, and especially, those who have the means to contribute a lot to make it happen. They want to know what and why. I ask, "If a wealthy person came up to you and asked, 'Why would I give your church a large donation?' you'd better have an answer that moves the hand to write a check!" Money follows vision, not the other way around.

It took a while, but eventually, Vincent had uncovered something in his heart that hadn't been connected to the needs in the community. When the connection was made, oh my, what a difference! Vincent worked with the people on his team to hear their stories and connect their hearts with God's heart and the needs in the community. Many of them jumped at the opportunity to make Vincent's vision for men a reality. They had their own twist on it, but that was fine with Vincent. He wanted them to have a heartfelt passion just like he did.

In a recent conversation with Vincent, he told me about the need to hire an additional staff member. He had met with a person with excellent skills, but he told me, "Chris, I'm not sure he'd fit in our culture."

I wanted to say, "Hey, look at how far you've come!" But I just smiled and nodded.

Every leader has a God-ordained passion, often latent and waiting to be discovered. I'm convinced that when they find it, they'll blow the doors off to make it happen. For instance, as I met with a pastor in another city, I went through many of the same exercises that I used with Vincent and Katrina. I asked, "What are people in the city afraid of? What makes them anxious?"

EVERY LEADER HAS A GOD-ORDAINED PASSION, OFTEN LATENT AND WAITING TO BE DISCOVERED.

The answers came fast and furiously: they're worried about the impact of the culture on their kids. The pastor and the people on the team were concerned about the city, and specifically, the young people who were being inundated with social media, music, and images that led them far from God. As we talked several times, the vision surfaced that this church could be the premier site where parents could bring their kids, specifically teenagers, to experience the life-changing power of God's love. They got creative and thought of ways they could partner with schools to provide facilities, resources, and mentoring for kids in junior high and high school. Then they got to work: making calls, creating programs, recruiting volunteers, and finding resources. That dream has become a reality. No, they haven't touched all the kids in the city, but God has used them to bring hope, love, and purpose to hundreds of kids—and a lot more peace for their parents.

THINK ABOUT IT:

What is your church's mission statement?

What's the vision statement?

What strategies are working well?

How would you identify your church's core, aspirational, and accidental values?

EVALUATE: Which of the exercises in this chapter might work well for you and your team?

EDUCATE: Who needs the exercises explained so they make a difference?

ESTABLISH: What's your first step?

EXECUTE: How will you make real progress?

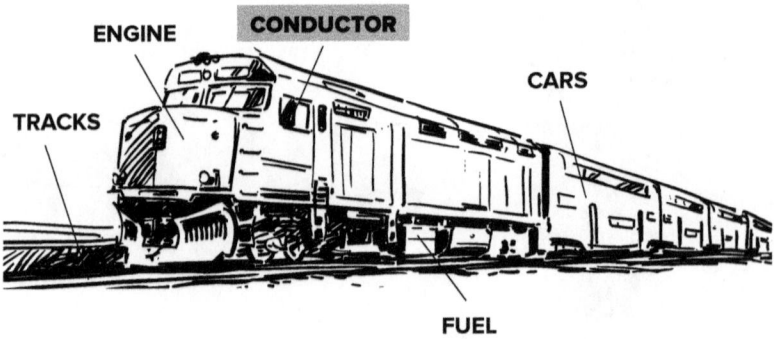

ENGINE

CONDUCTOR

CARS

TRACKS

FUEL

CHAPTER 5

CONDUCTOR: THE ESSENTIAL ROLE OF THE PASTOR

The conductor symbolizes the senior pastor's role in guiding the ministry. In this chapter, we'll explore the essential responsibilities of this crucial leadership position, including visionary leadership, shepherding the congregation, and providing spiritual guidance. By focusing on the core functions, pastors will enhance their effectiveness and influence within the church and in the wider community.

The life of a train conductor is often as bizarre as being a pastor, with similarly strange stories. A man who worked on the Pittsburgh rail system was onboard when a deer jumped out of the woods in front of the train—which was traveling at fifty miles an hour. The deer didn't have a chance against the massive engine. The conductor immediately got on his radio and contacted someone he called "Hannibal Lecter," giving the person the milepost number. After the train finished its run and turned around, the conductor looked outside and saw a man in full camouflage gear butchering the deer. The two men looked at each other and waved.[8] The things you do for your friends.

I'VE FOUND THAT THE VAST MAJORITY OF THEM ARE WONDERFUL PEOPLE WHO NEED SOME NEW TOOLS, A NEW SKILL OR TWO, AND SOME FRESH STRATEGIC IDEAS.

As I've consulted with hundreds (and maybe thousands) of pastors over the past decade, I've found that the vast majority of them are wonderful people who need some new tools, a new skill or two, and some fresh strategic ideas. A few contact me because they're drowning in staff conflict, and nothing they've tried has worked, or they have other relational or personal problems that need outside attention.

GETTING UNSTUCK

Mike and Ashley pastor a mid-sized church near Portland, Oregon. A friend of theirs had heard me speak at a conference and referred me to them. In our introductory conversation, Mike told me he felt stuck—not only that the church wasn't

---

8 Rosa Pasquarella, "Train Conductors Describe the Creepiest Things They've Seen," *Ranker*, Ranker, 23 Mar. 2020, www.ranker.com/list/creepy-railroad-stories/rosa-pasquarella.

growing like he hoped it would, but the team wasn't functioning very well. We talked about me coming for an onsite visit, but as I always do, I explained, "I want to make sure we're a good fit for you and you're a good fit for us. We don't want to waste time or money."

As we continued to talk, he was convinced he needed my help. He explained, "I need someone to take a hard look at what's going on here and give me an evaluation."

I found time to spend a day at their church. I conducted an evaluation using our Discovery form and interviewed Mike, Ashley, and the staff members. Mike told me, "Yeah, I'm not sure I have the right people on our team. They're lazy, and it doesn't seem they're committed to what we're trying to do. When I present ideas or new programs, they're resistant. It seems we can't make any progress because of them."

That statement was at least a yellow flag—if not a bright red one! I instantly realized there was more than a little tension between Mike and a number of people on the team, but I couldn't put my finger on it in the first hour with Mike. I then spent forty to forty-five minutes with each of the people on the team, four full-time staff members, and a couple of part-timers. Actually, I was pretty impressed with them. They told me about their backgrounds and their roles, and in different ways, they told me about their love for the people in their church. But I could tell all was not well with the team. I went back a couple of other times and spent more time with the staff team. I asked them to take personality/temperament inventories to see where they and Mike might be missing each other.

When I went back and met with them again, I asked, "What do you like most about the church?" They had a lot of good things to say. Then I asked, "What do you like least? What would you like to see changed?" I let the question sink in for a few seconds, and then I reframed it: "If your team walked in tomorrow morning, turned on the lights, and you were the lead pastor, what are the first two or three things you'd change?" This is an exercise I call "First Day Experience," and it invariably produces a world of insights.

When they tell me what they'd change, I ask, "Do you think any of the others on the team would make the same changes?" This question lets them be even more honest because they can share their own views through the voices of other people. I sometimes double down: "If I went to the other staff and asked what frustrates them the most about being on the team, what do you think they'd tell me?"

At Mike and Ashley's church, some common themes surfaced from these conversations: those on the team genuinely loved the people at the church, but they felt they needed to walk on eggshells around Mike. They tried to be positive about him, but as I pressed a little, the picture became clear: Mike was very insecure, he was threatened by gifted people who were praised by others, he had to be right all the time, and his way to put people in their place was using snarky, passive-aggressive statements disguised as humor. He was conflict-avoidant, but his coping strategy of talking *about* people but not *to* them created much more conflict and hurt feelings. When the youth group began to explode in growth, suddenly, most of the youth pastor's requests for space and resources were denied. It was Mike's way of making sure no one's star eclipsed his own.

I knew I was in a dilemma: If I spoke up about Mike's insecurity, I was pretty sure he'd blow up, blame me and his team for not being supportive, and I'd lose any chance to make a difference in their lives. But if I took the easy way out and talked only about strategies and tools, I would abdicate my God-given calling—and I'd be a coward. As always, I asked the Lord to give me wisdom to speak the right words at the right time in the right way.

Thankfully, Mike asked me to share my observations about him and the team. This was the open door I'd been looking for. And I did: I communicated my observations but not the input from the people on the team. I wanted to protect them from any backlash, and besides, they'd shared their perspectives confidentially, and I wanted to respect that.

Mike and I went to lunch. I asked for a table in the back where we could have privacy. I began by saying, "I appreciate you asking me to be honest with you. I want to return the favor: I want you to be honest with me. We'll get a lot farther that way." He nodded his agreement, and away we went. I asked him to tell me about his family background, and he told me about his very strained relationship with his father who had been verbally and physically abusive. His mother had been supportive, but if anything, too supportive—she'd smothered him with attention to make up for the lack of love from his dad. I asked, "How do you think those relationships affected you?"

A COACH ASKS QUESTIONS TO FACILITATE SELF-DISCOVERY; A CONSULTANT PROVIDES SOLUTIONS. SOMETIMES, THE ROLES SWITCH SEVERAL TIMES IN ANY SITUATION.

(I have master's degrees in leadership and coaching, but I consider myself a consultant, not a coach. A coach asks questions to facilitate self-discovery; a consultant provides solutions. In this conversation, I flipped roles several times between coaching and consulting. It was the only way to get where I knew we needed to go.)

Mike and I talked for two hours, and I think he was able to connect some dots between the hurts and fears of his childhood and his current defensive behavior with his team. He had been living under a cloud of self-doubt and unresolved emotional pain. His mother's smothering had robbed him of confidence, giving him the unintended message, "You can't make it on your own."

I asked Mike, "How do you think that pain and those messages have affected your marriage to Ashley and your relationship with your kids?" We talked about that for a while, and then I asked, "And how do they affect how you lead your team?" He said he wasn't sure, so I asked, "What do you imagine they feel during staff meetings when you squash their ideas?"

Ahh, maybe they weren't lazy and resistant after all. Maybe they were guarding themselves against unfair (and unspoken but very real) accusations. He told me, "I think I suck all the oxygen out of the room. I kill their creativity and motivation."

Mike was beginning to see clear patterns that had dominated his life since he was a kid. In that two-hour conversation, he allowed himself to feel more pain, anger, fear, and shame than ever before. It wasn't pretty, but it was absolutely necessary. I recommended a very good Christian counselor to him, and he made an appointment on the spot.

As we left the restaurant, I suggested, "Let's meet on Zoom twice a month instead of just once. One of those times we'll talk about your progress dealing with past hurts, and the other time we'll talk about ministry strategy."

"Sounds good," he responded.

Of course, it wasn't up to me to tell the team any of this. He could tell them when and if he was ready, which wasn't going to be very soon. In the meantime, I continued to travel to their city to meet with them. I used the Boxes and Batons exercise, as well as a few others. They ate it up! Each time, someone on the team told me on the way to the airport as I left, "Chris, when you're in the room, we can talk about strategies and timing and responsibilities. We feel encouraged, and even excited. When you're not in the room. . . ."

But things weren't completely rosy. From time to time in those staff meetings, when I presented an idea for them to consider, Mike solemnly announced, "I'm not sure about that." Several times, he told the team (and me) after I shared a strategic idea, "Yeah, I did that at my church twenty years ago. The program I led went really well. Good call, Chris." Was this affirmation? No, not really. He was threatened that his team valued me, and in his mind, more than they valued him, so he was using every trick to stay on top, even to subtly say, "Chris's idea isn't anything new. I did that years ago."

Each time this happened, I looked around the room to see how the people on the team were responding, and each time, I saw eyes rolled, slight head shakes, and faint smiles that said, "There he goes again!"

I looked for the right times to privately point out what I'd seen in Mike's false bravado. On my next visit, I asked him to meet with just me for breakfast, and we'd have the staff meeting a little later in the morning. Again, I held up a mirror, pointing out what he'd said and done. To his credit, he admitted he had felt threatened each time the team looked excited when I was leading them. Now he had one more thing to bring up in his meetings with the counselor!

Over the next several months, the vibe of the team changed dramatically. It wasn't that Mike had been instantly healed of his emotional wounds, but he was now aware of his defensiveness—and the source of it in his wounded heart. His perception made him more humble, less critical, and a better listener. He still made some snarky comments, and after the meetings, I asked, "Mike, how do you think people felt when you said that?"

He usually responded, "At least, frustrated with me and probably angry. And I don't blame them."

The first of the ninety-five theses Martin Luther nailed to the church door in Wittenberg said that for the Christian, all of life is repentance. That's what Mike was learning. The defensive patterns were deeply ingrained in his mind and heart, but he was learning to repent often and well. It made a huge difference—to him and in his most important relationships.

After about six months, Mike told the staff team that he had been seeing a counselor. He explained some of his childhood trauma, but he didn't tell them everything—yet. Mike wept as he shared his experiences. The people in the room listened, and when he was done, they were incredibly supportive. They were ready to take a bullet for Mike!

I was there. When Mike finished, and the people on the team expressed their love for him, I told them, "Mike has made some huge strides in the last few months, but like all of us, he's a work in progress. He's still going to say things that frustrate you. Talk to him after the meeting and tell him how you felt when he said this or that. If you'll be patient with him and stay engaged, some amazing things will happen in the lives of everyone on the team."

Mike turned to them and said, "Hey, guys, I really need your help. Tell me when I'm over the line."

I jumped in to explain to the team, "That's your invitation to be involved in a way that changes lives: Mike's and your own. Don't settle for artificial harmony, and don't be mean. There's a lot of room in the middle between those two!"

By the end of the first year, God had done amazing things in Mike's life and the culture of the team. They had actually become a team instead of a boss and some cogs in his machine. Everyone on the team had grown in the beautiful blend of humility and boldness. By the second year, we implemented some structures and strategies to grow the church, and it grew by about 50 percent.

It was my great honor to consult with them for three years. I spoke there not long ago, and it was a wonderful experience to see the ways God had worked, first in Mike, then the team, and then throughout the church. I don't know much about brain surgery, but I think the doctor makes sure he doesn't touch some parts when he's working on others. That's how I felt consulting, coaching, and occasionally counseling Mike—I wanted to be very careful not to touch certain things too much too soon.

I coached by being involved with the whole team, asking good questions to see what they see. Then I could bring things up to Mike in a bold yet sensitive way because I'd seen the same things. I could then coach Mike by asking questions so that he discovered the deep truths about himself. At that point, I did a little counseling and then referred him to a professional. After that, I could go back to my sweet spot as a consultant, listening, offering ideas, and gently prodding them to take action.

CHECKING THE OIL

The conductor on a train isn't the engineer, but sometimes, the engineer needs to do some diagnostics with the conductor to see if he's functioning well. With Mike, I was the engineer, and I used a bunch of tools to uncover some things that had been hidden for years.

THE CONDUCTOR ON A TRAIN ISN'T THE ENGINEER, BUT SOMETIMES, THE ENGINEER NEEDS TO DO SOME DIAGNOSTICS WITH THE CONDUCTOR TO SEE IF HE'S FUNCTIONING WELL.

First Day Experience

I use this exercise to uncover the frustrations of team members. It's a simple but poignant question that I ask individually: "If your team walked in tomorrow morning, turned on the lights, and you were the lead pastor, what are the first two or three things you'd change?"

It doesn't take long for them to answer because they've been thinking about this for months or even years. The way the question is framed doesn't demean the pastor, but it gives each person the opportunity to express genuine concerns about the pastor's leadership, the strategies employed, the quality of their relationships, and the way they feel both directed and valued—or not. I don't share their responses with anyone else. Their answers are just for me to get a good read on what's going on with the team. If I observe similar things in my interactions with the pastor, I can bring those up in our conversations.

Quick Looks

When teams aren't functioning well, I often use instruments to identify personality and temperament traits. A number of them have been used successfully for years, including the Myers-Briggs Personality Assessment, the DiSC Assessment, and the Enneagram. These aren't clinical evaluations, but they often give a good snapshot of the way people feel and act, especially under pressure. Quite often, I find that at least some of the conflict on a team is the result of misunderstanding, and when people find out what makes others tick, they're more patient and supportive.

Likable, Capable, Gravitational

Early in our conversations, Mike told me, "I need your help with something. It's hard for us to attract and keep quality staff members." That kind of comment always is an indicator of a deeper problem. I explained that there are three levels of relational leadership:

Pastors can be *likable.* They're good-natured, can tell a good joke, like sports, and generally are fun to be around. It may surprise you, but Mike was very likable—unless you were on his team. Some people are distant until you get to know them, and then they're quite likable, but others are likable until you get to know them, and then you find out they're not really safe. Mike was in the second category. I explained, "Mike, I gotta be honest with you. There are lots of people who love to be around you, but the closer the proximity, the less likable you are. When people are close, they feel you try to control them instead of loving them. Do you understand what I'm saying?"

He did, and my observation led to a huge step of self-realization.

Pastors can be both *likable and capable*. These pastors are likable enough to draw people close, and they've also demonstrated talent in leading, speaking, organizing, administrating, or other capabilities. Mike was a gifted speaker, but because he wasn't likable, his leadership and administration had been hindered.

Pastors can be *likable, capable, and gravitational*. The sun's gravitational force keeps the planets in orbit in our solar system. Without that pull, they'd drift off into the distant reaches of the universe. A gravitational leader not only draws people close, but like the sun, he gives light and energy to them. These pastors believe in people, and they know it. They give enough direction, and they encourage people to reach their full potential.

Gravitational pastors are *looking for* the right *who* for their team, but they're also committed to *being* the right *who* for each person who reports to them. These leaders see themselves as coaches, bringing out the best in each person orbiting around them. These pastors aren't threatened by others' talents and success. In fact, they live to make others successful and celebrate every triumph. They provide resources, connect people to a broader network of other leaders, and become their biggest cheerleaders.

IT'S SHORTSIGHTED FOR PASTORS TO THINK ONLY OF THE VALUE THEIR TEAM MEMBERS ADD TO THEIR OWN MINISTRIES; INSTEAD, THEY CONSCIOUSLY AND CONTINUALLY ADD VALUE TO EACH PERSON ON THE TEAM.

Gravitational pastors are experts at imparting a compelling vision for the church, for each team member, and for the team as they work together to accomplish far more than the sum of their efforts. It's shortsighted for pastors to think only of the value their team members add to their own ministries; instead, they consciously and continually add value to each person on the team. Zig Ziglar was one of my favorite leadership experts. He once said, "You will get all you want in life if you help enough people get what they want."[9]

I shared Zig's quote with Mike, and I told him, "Connect people to a big vision, and do all you can to help them thrive and succeed. When you become their raving fan, they'll want to be near you. It will be the most fulfilling thing you'll ever do in your life. Some people do it naturally, but others have to work hard to learn how to add value to others. You can

9   Kevin Kruse, "Zig Ziglar: 10 Quotes That Can Change Your Life," *Forbes*, 12 Sept. 2023, https://www.forbes.com/sites/kevinkruse/2012/11/28/zig-ziglar-10-quotes-that-can-change-your-life/?sh=4032114f26a0.

CONDUCTOR: THE ESSENTIAL ROLE OF THE PASTOR

learn the skill." I knew it was in Mike's heart to be his team's cheerleader. It would take some time to learn how, but it was obvious he really wanted to play that role in their lives.

I wanted to give Mike a personal example of how a leader can change. I shared, "About twenty years ago, my best friend took me aside and said, 'Chris, I love you like a brother, but there are two things you need to know."

I responded with a measure of anxiety: "Okay, I'm listening."

"First, you speak before you think, and your words sometimes hurt people. A quick wit is fine, as long as it's guided by love."

I nodded. I knew he was right. I braced myself for the second blow.

He continued, "The look on your face says you're always angry."

I wanted to give him a dozen excuses. I wanted to tell him he was wrong. I wanted to find a way for him to back down from what he'd said—but I knew he was right. I was deeply hurt by his courageous observations, but at that moment, I decided to go to war against the enemies he'd identified. It wasn't enough to acknowledge that change was needed; I was committed to doing whatever it took to change.

A few months later, I saw my friend, and he said, "Hey, Chris, you're smiling!"

I showed him a sticky note I kept on a book I was carrying (that was before cell phones) that said, "Smile!" Another one said, "Encourage!"

He laughed and said, "Whatever it takes!"

It was in my heart to affirm people, to be an encouragement to them, to be a light of hope when they went through hard times, but for years, my heart hadn't connected with my face. I was determined to make that connection, and I was willing to move heaven and earth to have a more positive impact on people. It was an exercise in continual repentance. I messed up over and over again, and I still mess up, but I've made a ton of progress. Today, most people wouldn't think that I ever wore "a mad face." When I speak at churches, many pastors introduce me by saying something like this: "Chris is every pastor's raving fan!" If they only knew. I hadn't been very likable. I was capable but not likable, and if you're not likable, you're certainly not going to be gravitational! If I was going to have a positive impact for the kingdom, I had to make some major changes. I had to go to war.

I told Mike, "It's time to suit up and go to war! It's not enough to settle for marginal gains that allow you to easily drift back into old habits. Do the work. Make the effort. Put reminders on your phone, on your mirror, and on your desk to remind you to see every person as a treasure to value. Ask a person or two to hold you accountable, and don't let them off the hook."

To drive the point home, I asked, "How many times do you look at your phone each day?"

"About two hundred, I guess."

"Great. Make 'Add value' your screen saver, so you have two hundred reminders every day."

Mike announced, "I'll do it!"

And he did. I spoke there not long ago, and the entire mood of the church is different than it was when I first stepped into Mike's office. People are friendly, they're committed to the mission, and they love each other. They're becoming like their pastor. Mike became gravitational.

Mission Critical

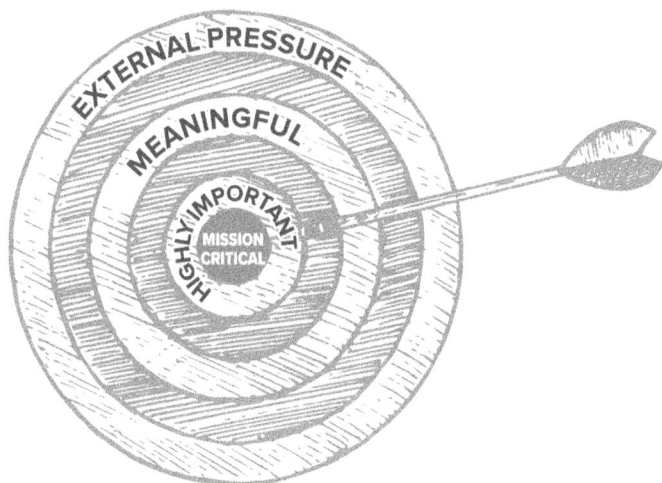

This exercise focuses the pastor's attention on what will move the church forward. I didn't use this with Mike and his team until almost a year after we met, but when we used it, it made a big impact.

WE NEED TO TRADE A LOT OF OUR TIME SPENT ON URGENT THINGS FOR THE ACTIVITIES THAT MATTER FAR MORE.

When Mike's heart began to heal and his team began to function more effectively, I told Mike, "Man, I'm so proud of the progress I see. You're so courageous to deal with the pain you've suffered, and your team is much more energized and effective. But Mike, you and your team members have a problem that's common to many of us: you can't differentiate between the *urgent* and the *important.* You're running around frantically doing things that seem urgent, but you're neglecting things that are more important." I began with a simple but helpful statement: "You can't add hours; you can only trade them." I explained that they needed to trade a lot of their time spent on urgent things for the activities that matter far more.

People always ask, "But Chris, how can I tell if something is mission critical?"

"Easy," I respond. "Just complete this sentence: If I don't do _____, our future is threatened." The senior pastor needs to fill in the blank, but so does every other person on the team. This is the most important exercise I do with people. It gives them insight into their mission, and it clarifies their efforts to fulfill it every single day.

I said, "Mike, would counseling go in the blank? If you don't do counseling, is the future of the church threatened?"

He laughed, "No, I don't counsel people much at all."

"How about preaching every Sunday?"

"No, others can preach."

"How about leading every meeting?"

"No, certainly not."

"Do you see that those are important, but they're not mission critical?"

Mike nodded.

I explained, "You can't have more than three or four in the center of the target, the activities that are truly mission critical."

I told him, "The outside ring is external pressure. For instance, a person in the church calls you and says, 'Pastor Mike, I wish you'd preach verse by verse.' Someone else corners you in the hallway and asks, 'Why don't we have more ministries for women?' Another person tells you with a lot of emotion, 'Pastor, the world is going to hell. Why aren't we more involved in the community?' 'We should have different songs on Sunday.' 'We should be more Pentecostal.' 'We should be less Pentecostal.' You get the idea. All of these are forms of external pressure."

Mike laughed and said, "I get these comments, emails, or calls after church every week!"

"Do you give in?" I asked.

Mike smiled and nodded. "Yeah, too often."

"What are your reasons?"

He thought for a few seconds, and then he told me, "I don't want people to think I don't care. I don't want the conflict that would come if they think I don't care. And I don't want the person to spread dissension if he thinks I don't care." A few seconds later, he added, "And often, the pressure comes from our biggest givers, and I certainly don't want to offend them! If they want us to do more for the hungry and homeless, it's easy to say, 'Okay, we're on it!'"

The next circle is "meaningful." I shared, "These are the things you like to do, and they're productive, but they're not mission critical."

"Like what?" Mike asked.

"Let me give you an example: I consulted with a pastor who had been a singer in a rock group before he became a believer. When I went to his church on a Sunday morning, at a church of about four hundred, guess who was leading worship? Yep, the pastor. He loved it, but the preparation took time away from more important work he needed to do every week."

The third level is "highly important" which includes a range of activities that are really important, but they don't go in the blank of threatening the future of the church if they're not done. This level includes preaching, teaching, leading the staff, the website, graphics, making sure the electricity stays on, and so on.

I leaned in: "Let me give you another example: A youth pastor told me he picks up a different kid each day after school to grab some frozen yogurt and shoot some hoops. He spends a couple of hours with a different kid each day. The church is growing like crazy, but the youth group has fifty of his biggest fans. When I talked to him about it, he insisted, 'The kids love it, and it's what their parents want me to do.' Mike, what's wrong with this picture?"

He chimed in: "He was doing a highly important thing with those kids, but he wasn't giving enough attention to mission-critical activities."

"Exactly. One more example: Imagine being at LAX with twenty-five thousand people waiting to get on their flights. An announcement says, 'We're sorry to inform you, but the water main has broken, and there's no water in the airport.' The maintenance people scramble to try to fix it. It seems like the most important thing in the world. After all, twenty-five thousand people can't go to the bathroom! But now imagine another announcement two minutes later, 'Ladies and gentlemen, we just learned that air traffic control has lost power, and we can't track any planes that are trying to land.' Mike, where do you think the attention of the airport officials will go? Which of these problems is highly important, and which is mission critical?"

"I get it!" Mike almost yelled. "The water looked like it was mission critical . . . until air traffic control lost power."

I was sure Mike understood the concept, so I took the concept back to the Gospels: "Theologians say that Jesus spent 60 to 70 percent of His waking hours with the disciples. Why did He devote that much time to them when there were so many sick and crippled (and dead!) people in the cities where He traveled?"

Mike jumped in, "Because building them to lead the church after He ascended was mission critical for Him."

JESUS HAD TO FOCUS HIS TIME AND HIS ENERGY ON WHAT WAS MOST IMPORTANT—NOT JUST MEANINGFUL, NOT JUST HIGHLY IMPORTANT, BUT THE THINGS THAT WERE MISSION CRITICAL.

"Precisely. The Gospels record only a handful of times when Jesus ate, but we can assume He ate every day except for the forty days He was tempted in the desert. And there's not one reference to Him going to the bathroom. I think we can say that happened plenty of times." Mike laughed. "The one thing we have in common with Jesus is that the perfect Son of God was limited to the same twenty-four hours a day that we have. His responsibilities and the demands on Him were infinitely bigger than what we live under, but the Father didn't give Him twenty-five hours, so He could do a little more. Like us, He had to focus His time and His energy on what was most important—not just meaningful, not just highly important, but the things that were mission critical. He had to make choices every day to prioritize that. Actually, we can say Jesus had two things on His mission-critical list: He had to die to pay the penalty for our sins, and He had to prepare His disciples to launch the church."

I let that sink in for a few seconds, and then I told Mike: "If Jesus had said 'yes' to meaningful and highly important things, you and I wouldn't be sitting here today talking about Him, and through Him, the local church being the hope of the world." I closed the book on this by telling Mike, "Jesus had to say 'no' to a lot of really good things because He couldn't add more hours to His days. He could only trade His hours for the things that were genuinely mission critical. Time is the great equalizer—for Jesus and for you and me."

Mike responded, "Okay, how do I determine what's mission critical for me?"

"That's the right question. You need to wrestle with it, so you develop strong convictions about what's of ultimate importance to you, but let me give you some tracks to run on." This is the exercise I used with Mike and one I use with a lot of pastors:

1] Take the next two or three weeks to think and pray, and then send me a list of the three or four activities that are mission critical for you. This fills in the blank, "If I don't do _____, our future is threatened."

2] After that, make a list of everything you currently do at the church, and I mean everything: preparing to preach, Sunday mornings, emails, meetings, and everything else you do daily, weekly, monthly, quarterly, and yearly. Everything. You may have fifty to one hundred items on the list, maybe more.

3] Make a list with three or four headings that are each of your mission-critical activities, and put the items on the long list you just made under the headings. This tells you which of your activities actually contribute to what's mission critical for you. The objective is to place activities in one of the mission-critical lists. Don't force it. If one doesn't fit, leave it on the unassigned list. In most cases, pastors have a lot left over! In fact, you might have twenty-five or more left on your list after this portion of the exercise.

4] Now, make a list of the leftovers. For each one, determine if you can eliminate, delegate, or automate the activity so it's no longer on your to-do list. Do what you need to do to take those off your plate, and let me tell you: Be ruthless! You'll find plenty of excuses to keep them, and you'll disappoint some people when they realize their pet project is no longer your priority. Do you think Jesus disappointed some people? Yeah, a lot of times.

5] Now, write a plan to maximize the impact of each of your mission-critical activities. Carve out 60 to 70 percent of your time to devote to those things. Undoubtedly, the transition will require some mid-course corrections to be sure you stay focused. Maybe you need to delegate more things, maybe you need to eliminate one or two that had stayed on the list, or maybe you have someone who can automate a task or two. The point is this: don't stop tweaking until your focus and your schedule are consistently on the mission-critical elements in your role. If there are some left over, that's perfectly okay. Put those on the "highly important" list.

One pastor told me that one of his mission-critical elements is "to develop high-functioning teams."

I responded, "That's great. What activities will get you there?"

He responded, "Let's see . . . creating a process of recruiting, training, placing, and overseeing people on these teams, and another part would be raising up competent, gifted, focused leaders who can multiply themselves in the lives of those who join the teams."

I replied, "You've got it. The building blocks are essential, so you have enough great teams to enable growth. You said you want to start two new campuses in the next year. Where will those leaders come from? Recruiting, training, placing, and overseeing men and women who are committed to Christ and His cause." I paused for a second and then asked, "So, what are the consequences of not doing these mission-critical activities?"

His eyes widened, and he remarked, "Our future is threatened."

I continued, "Building effective teams is the result of the mission-critical activities of noticing rising leaders, creating a team culture, putting a vision in front of each person that captures their hearts, showing them how their part has a huge impact on the mission of the church, being shrewd in selecting team leaders who have this heart and this vision, celebrating the teams often and genuinely, and keeping all this in the 60 to 70 percent of your time because it's a mission-critical priority." I pressed a little more. "What has to happen for your guest relations team to be outstanding? What has to happen for your small group leaders to be effective shepherds of the people in their groups? And the worship team, and the kids' ministry, and the youth group, and on and on throughout the church? If having great teams is mission critical, devote enough time and effort to it—and make sure nothing takes your time away from it."

I may not use this exercise from day 1 in my interactions with a pastor and the team, but sooner or later, I take it out of the toolkit. It's amazingly helpful in creating traction. Sometimes, my initial focus is on conflict resolution, a lack of vision, or insecurity; the conductor often needs some personal attention before we talk about other parts of the train. But if the pastor needs tools, skills, and strategies to recharge growth, we get to this exercise pretty quickly.

THINK ABOUT IT:

What are some ways to determine if a church or a staff team is stuck because of a personal issue with the conductor or if it's the need to implement different strategies?

When a person is fragile and defensive (though he or she may not appear to be fragile at all), what are some good ways to address the problem?

What might be some benefits of using the "First Day Experience" exercise with your team? Do you think they'd be honest with you? Why or why not?

After reading this chapter, how would you describe the conductor's role?

EVALUATE: Which of the exercises in this chapter might work well for you and your team?

EDUCATE: Who needs the exercises explained, so they make a difference?

ESTABLISH: What's your first step?

EXECUTE: How will you make real progress?

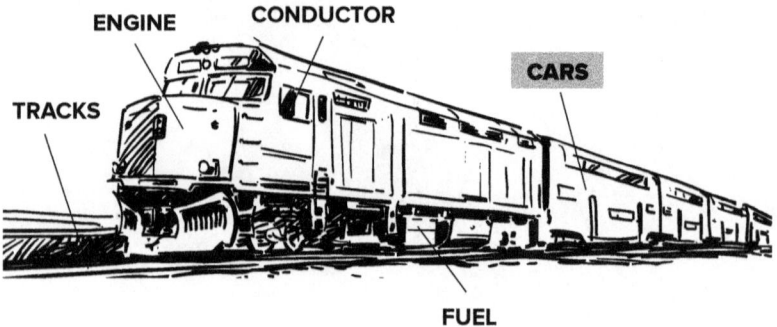

ENGINE

CONDUCTOR

CARS

TRACKS

FUEL

CHAPTER 6

CARS: ALIGNMENT OF STAFF, LEADERS, AND THE CONGREGATION

The train cars represent the various components of the ministry, including staff members, key volunteer leaders, and the congregation. Pastors need to align these vital elements, so the church functions cohesively as a unified body. Through effective communication, team-building, and shared vision, pastors foster an environment of cooperation and collaboration.

Most rail cars have a gross weight of about 286,000 pounds, and some can weigh 315,000 pounds. In comparison, the weight limit for trucks on interstate highways is eighty thousand pounds, so one train car takes the place of about 3.5 trucks The newest locomotives are equipped with supercomputers that can process a billion data points per second, enabling them to improve the efficiency of hauling cars filled with goods of all kinds.[10] Trains derail for a number of reasons: collisions with other trains or at crossings with cars or trucks, conductor error, track failure, broken rails, or defective parts of the cars, such as axles and wheels.

In the most recent statistics, the Bureau of Transportation Statistics reported almost two thousand derailments a year.[11] killing at least one person every 100 minutes, or about 1,000 annually. Recent train derailments have made national news, but perhaps the worst rail accident in our nation's history occurred on July 9, 1918, when two trains collided at 60 mph at "Dutchman's Curve" between Nashville and Memphis.[12] The impact killed 101 people and seriously injured 171. The disaster happened because of a miscommunication between train operators that left both trains barreling toward each other on the same track. The cars in a church's train can derail for a number of reasons too. One of the most common is an unclear vision. I tell pastors, "In the absence of clarity, people arrive at their own conclusions." Miscommunication (or the lack of communication) leaves a leadership vacuum. Some people fill in the blanks and press ahead with their own agendas, others become confused and passive because they don't want to make a mistake, and a few use this opportunity to gossip and blame everybody for the chaos. Sometimes, people's strengths and passion don't fit the role they occupy,

---

10 "12 Train Facts You Might Not Know," *Union Pacific*, 29 Mar. 2022, www.up.com/customers/track-record/tr030822-12-train-facts-you-might-not-know.htm.
11 Kelly Jones, "Yes, the US Averages More than 1,700 Train Derailments a Year," *Verifythis.Com*, 1 Mar. 2023, www.verifythis.com/article/news/verify/national-verify/us-averages-more-than-1700-train-derailments-a-year-fact-check/536-a3d9e66c-b24a-4f16-a3a2-262942d50ec8.
12 Alex Denis and Caitlin Huff, "Dutchman's Curve Train Crash 'worst Disaster' in Nashville's History," *WKRN News 2*, 24 June 2022, www.wkrn.com/special-reports/hidden-tn/dutchmans-curve-train-crash-worst-disaster-in-nashvilles-history/.

financial problems can create enormous stress among leaders, values aren't clearly stated—or worse, they're stated but not followed—or theological or cultural differences can cause conflict. For all of these, the erosion or the shattering of trust is often the painful consequence of misalignment.

THE EROSION OR THE SHATTERING OF TRUST IS OFTEN THE PAINFUL CONSEQUENCE OF MISALIGNMENT.

To be aligned, the pastor needs to be sure everybody on the train understands and is committed to the mission, vision, values, goals, and roles. I often use the Riverbanks exercise to help teams clarify these things. Without clear and strong banks, the church becomes a placid pond—little vision, little passion, little effectiveness—but pleasant! Clarifying and strengthening these necessary elements can turn that pond back into a dynamic, raging, effective river.

ONE OF THE WORST

When I met Jamal and Vanessa, their church near Atlanta was large, about eight hundred on an average Sunday, with four hundred in small groups. They had ten full-time staff members and a few part-time. Jamal called to ask for my help, and he explained, "Chris, we're just not growing. I know we have a lot more potential, but we seem to have hit a ceiling. I need some help with our strategies. Would you help us?"

I scheduled a day to fly in to visit with Jamal, Vanessa, and their team. As always, I spent the day listening to the history of the church and evaluating the team, the structures and strategies, and Jamal's leadership. And as I always do, I met with people on the team. I didn't have time to spend forty to forty-five minutes with everybody, so I asked six of them to meet with me.

When I met with Jamal and Vanessa early in the day, they again stressed that they needed help with structures and strategy. If they even mentioned the staff team, I don't remember it. But later that day, as I met with several of the people on the team, I got a very different picture: two of them had deep resentments toward Jamal. They believed he had misled them about their roles, passed over them when they asked to fill a slot left open by someone leaving the team, and was taking them for granted. But that wasn't the worst of it.

When I talked to Carl, the executive pastor, an enormous amount of venom spilled out! I asked him to tell me what had caused the break in their relationship, and he gave me a detailed history of Jamal's inattention and public criticisms. He told me he only found out what Jamal really thought of him when others told me what Jamal had said to them. I asked the obvious question, "Have you talked to him about your feelings and perceptions?"

Carl glared and said, "A dozen times."

"What happened?"

"Every time, he said he understood, and he apologized, but a week or two later, I heard the same thing again—he had blasted me to someone on the team, on the board, or in the church. After a while, I gave up."

"Do you know of anyone else on the team who has problems with Jamal?"

Carl leaned back and said, "Oh, man, everybody does."

"Everybody?"

"Well, two of them carry a lot of hurt because of Jamal."

"And you know this because. . . ."

"We're in the trenches together. We're a band of brothers trying to survive the battle. We support each other."

This told me the three of them had formed an alliance against Jamal. Was it justified in any way? I needed to find out, but first. . . ."Carl," I asked, "why are you still here?"

He grimaced and told me, "This is where my parents live, my wife's parents live, and where our kids are rooted in their schools and sports. I've put up with Jamal because of them."

I wanted to argue with him about his reasoning for staying at that particular church, but I wanted to hear the other side of the story from Jamal. Later that afternoon, I carefully related at least parts of my observations to Jamal, and I asked him, "Do you sense any tension between you and anyone on the team?"

"Not really. No, all good."

Actually, Jamaal was right, at least to some extent: a number of things were "all good" at the church. Sunday services went pretty well, so they were attracting a steady stream of people—just about the same number as those who left because they moved or found something a bit off at the church. And for some reason, the pastor attracted the generosity of a number of big givers. The church was awash in money in the bank. But there was rot in the heart of the church, and it needed to be cut out—the sooner, the better.

I learned that staff tensions had existed for more than two years, and from some offhand comments, I figured out that the impetus to ask for my help didn't originate with Jamal. A member of the board was so concerned about staff conflicts that he insisted Jamal make the call. Now I knew why Jamal said things were "all good": he didn't want me to delve too deeply into the morass of team relationships. From the standpoint of the community, the church was chugging along very well, but insiders were aware that some of the cars had already derailed, and a bigger, nastier crash was coming soon.

Before I left that first day with them, I had my recap meeting with Jamal and Vanessa. They asked what new strategies I recommended, and I responded, "We'll get to that at some point, but there's a different problem I want to discuss. Did you know that there are three people on your team who are creating all kinds of tension? They're talking to each other, they're talking to others on the team, and they're talking to people in the congregation. They're spreading the cancer of disunity throughout your church."

I barely got the last sentence out of my mouth when both of them nodded and said in unison, "Yes, we know all about it."

I asked, "How long have you known it?"

Vanessa said, "Almost two years."

"Then why haven't you done something about it? It's poison for your team."

"It's not really that bad, Chris."

"I have to disagree. From what I heard today, it requires emergency surgery."

I talked about how to confront the three and how to rebuild trust among the people who would be left on the team, but it appeared Jamal had drifted into outer space. I've known some conflict-avoidant pastors in my life, but not one who dissociated right in front of my eyes!

THE WORST THING YOU CAN DO TO A STRONG TEAM MEMBER IS TOLERATE A WEAK ONE. AND THE WORST THING YOU CAN DO TO FAITHFUL TEAM MEMBERS IS TOLERATE REBELS IN YOUR MIDST.

I used one of my favorite statements: "Jamal, I often tell pastors that the worst thing you can do to a strong team member is tolerate a weak one. In this case, the worst thing you can do to faithful team members is tolerate rebels in your midst. Your passivity is creating resentment and confusion among your best people. You've already lost a lot of leadership equity. People on your team are frustrated and confused—and those are the ones you need to keep! That needs to change."

During my conversations with the other people on the team, I had discovered that two staff members had left the church in the previous few months, and I suspected they just couldn't stand the toxic environment any longer. I then told Jamal and Vanessa another truth I've seen countless times: "Healthy churches cause unhealthy people to leave, but unhealthy churches cause healthy people to leave." I continued, "The constant, unresolved tension is lowering the productivity of every individual on the team, and worse, the lack of alignment has a multiplied, negative impact on the effectiveness of the church." I asked them to pray and think about that before our next meeting.

A month later, I was in their area, so I went to the church to meet with Jamal, Vanessa, and the team. As soon as I walked into the room, I noticed someone was missing: the executive pastor. For whatever reason, Carl realized it was in his best interests to jump ship, so he left a week or so after my first visit. With the rest of the team, I used the exercise "Right, Wrong, Missing, and Confusing" to let them identify the areas that needed attention. I asked them to be honest with me and with each other. A couple of them were hesitant to be vulnerable and take the risk, but most of them took advantage of the opportunity to say things they'd wanted to say for many months. It was important for Jamal and Vanessa to hear the people on their team share honestly with them. The executive pastor's departure was helpful, but it didn't solve all the problems.

One of them said, "I don't think we're being honest with each other."

Another said, "We don't do conflict well."

Still another commented, "We let things go when we need to address them."

Now it was out in the open. It became a problem for all of us to resolve together, but one person still wasn't on board: Pastor Jamal.

The next month, I traveled to be on-site with them, and I quickly realized my job that day was to be the HVAC technician: I needed to let them vent. There was too much hurt, too many times trust had been stomped on, and too much anger to start moving forward. It may have seemed unproductive to some people, but that's exactly what they needed.

By the following month's meeting, we were ready to deal with the issues: artificial harmony, conflict, hurt, resentment, and trust. I taught the process Jesus described in Matthew 18, and I was sure several of them would schedule appointments with the two who had been rebels before I arrived the first time. Some of them asked to have private conversations with Jamal.

The issues of misalignment were finally articulated and laid out on the table. They were beginning to understand one another, forgive one another, and trust one another. In one of the meetings in the following months, I asked them to get into groups of four and each person answer two questions: "What do you do that helps the team align and function well?" and "What do you do that contributes to misalignment?"

Jamal was finally ready to have heart-to-heart conversations with the two who had resented his leadership. By this time, Jamal realized that his inaction had contributed to the problem. He apologized and made a commitment to be more proactive. The two former detractors were glad to hear Jamal's new perspective, and they asked him to forgive them too. Humility and honesty made their talks much easier and more productive than they might have been.

COUNTLESS LITTLE THINGS, IF THEY AREN'T NOTICED AND ADDRESSED, CAN CAUSE A TRAIN (OR A CHURCH) TO DERAIL.

It was quite the effort to put the cars back on the track, so the train could move forward, but after about six months, we started talking about strategies that could help them grow.

When a train derails, the accident report almost invariably contains this statement: "The tragedy could have been avoid if. . . ." Usually, it's some grease on an axle, a signal light that should have been checked, or a crossing arm where the car should have stopped. Countless little things, if they aren't noticed and addressed, can cause a train (or a church) to derail. At that point, it takes a lot of manpower and some specialized machines to repair the tracks and put the cars back on the tracks. If only. . . .

To complete that sentence, we use these exercises:

Right, Wrong, Missing, Confusing

This allows the team to self-identify the obstacles on the tracks, which is far more motivating than having a consultant or pastor point them out. (See the explanation in chapter 3.)

Two Questions

This may be the simplest of the exercises in the book, but it's important. I use it with teams that are doing well, those that are in crisis, and those in between. In a staff meeting so they can hear and respond to each other, I ask them two questions: "What do you do that helps the team align and function well?" and "What do you do that contributes to misalignment?"

Their answers show the level of their understanding of the necessity of alignment, their assessment of the current condition of the team, and what they recommend as improvements. Quite often, a pastor has been trying to get team members aligned, but it's like "pushing cooked spaghetti up a hill." In this conversation, people on the team verbalize the problem, find solutions, and make commitments to the process of change.

Matthew 18 Every Week

When Jamal saw the benefits of following the model of conflict resolution in Matthew 18, he began every staff meeting by looking at the passage and asking, "Do any of us need to go to someone privately after the meeting today? If you do, do it—today. Don't wait. Do any of us have an ongoing conflict that needs two or three to mediate? If you do, ask wise people to help you. Don't wait. Do it today. Are any of us involved in a dispute that hasn't been resolved by the witness/mediators? If you are, let's talk about it now. The floor is open."

Did Jamal need to do this every week in the staff meeting? Yes, but more for himself to keep it on the front burner than for the rest of the team. The constant reminder helped the people on the team deal with small issues before they blew up into catastrophes, and Jamal learned the importance of honesty and vulnerability. This exercise was so effective that Jamal started using it at the beginning of his board meetings too.

4 X 4

This exercise is a natural outgrowth of Right, Wrong, Missing, Confusing, but now, we don't just talk; we make concrete plans. This is a way for every person on the team to align themselves with each other. It works like this:

Every four months, the team needs to determine four priorities to focus on. I led the discussion: "First, make a list of all the things that need attention in the next four months." They rattled off a lot of things and wrote them on the board. They included better guest relations, better follow-up of guests, building a strong leadership pipeline, community outreach, baptism classes, and on and on.

Then I asked, "Let's identify the four highest priorities. What has to happen for you to take the next step of growth?" This invariably produces interesting debates. They can get heated as people plead for their priority, but I tell them, "Do you see what's going on here? You're passionate about God's work in the lives of the people in your church and your community! There's nothing in the world wrong with having strong opinions, but we need to remember that we're in this together, and we're going to focus on four—just four. It's not that the others aren't important. They may just need to wait until the next four-month cycle."

Finally, they settled on four things: their not-very-sharp website, their leadership pipeline, an issue with the facilities (can't remember what that was), and recruiting more small group leaders for the next push for group involvement.

I circled these on the board. (We kept a list of the others so we could come back to them after the four-month cycle was over.) Then I said, "I always ask two questions at this point: Who needs to know it? Who needs to own it? How would you answer those questions?"

We looked at each of the four priorities and discussed who needed to know the team was making them a priority. For instance, who needed to know about the update for the website? They said, "All the department heads so they can feature what they're offering." "The board." "The media team, obviously."

"Okay," I told them. "Who needs to own it?"

They didn't have a tech expert on the team, but one of them had a friend who was a guru at crafting websites. "I'll work with him," he said. "I'll get a few of you to meet with him and me so we can talk about our goals, and then I'll ask him for a proposal." That was exactly the kind of ownership I was looking for.

Every week in their staff meeting, they had a status report about the four priorities: cooperation, progress, setbacks, questions, resources, and next steps. Each month, I was on

Zoom with the team, and they gave me reports about their progress. This kept us focused on the most important things they could do to have the biggest impact.

It was amazing. The team that had been so fragmented only months before showed the energy of synergy, and they loved working together to accomplish these goals. They had been bruised, and now they were acting like superheroes! If one of the four priorities wasn't completed, they carried it forward to the next four months.

I talk to pastors who drive themselves crazy by thinking of all the things they aren't doing. This exercise gives them the peace of focus. When they think of something else that needs to happen, they can put it on the list to talk about in the next four months. As Jamal would say, "All good"—but this time, it was true. And when people in the church ask staff members, "Why are we doing this and not that?" they can answer, "Great question. These are our four top priorities for the four months we're in now." If the person asks, "When are you going to focus on my this or that?" the staff member can say, "It's important. It's on the whiteboard at the office, and we'll get to it soon." This exercise enables every staff member to project confidence about the priorities of the team. Everyone owns the four for the next four months, everyone can explain them, and everyone can defend them. And the pastor doesn't feel like the Lone Ranger trying to deal with demands and criticisms coming from all directions.

By using the 4 X 4 exercise, the team develops a culture of mutual ownership of the projects and activities they've deemed most important for each four-month cycle. Culture always contains four levels: know, embrace, defend, and multiply. When I first met with Jamal and the team, they weren't even clear about what they needed to know and embrace, so they certainly weren't going to defend the priorities and multiply the impact. But as the team gelled and they used this powerful exercise, the culture of ownership became really strong. (Actually, it happened much faster than I expected.)

THERE'S NO REASON TO CHANGE EXERCISES THAT WORK WELL.

Jamal and Vanessa still start every meeting with Matthew 18, and they continue to have four-month cycles to focus on four priorities. No reason to change exercises that work so well.

Twelve-Week Year

Four by four is about the team's goals; this exercise is for the individuals on the team and is designed to help them stay focused on their goals, so they make real progress. We identify four twelve-week segments in the year (leaving out a few weeks for holidays). At Jamal and Vanessa's church, I sat down with each of the staff members and asked, "What do you want to accomplish over the next year?" One wanted to raise up more leaders, another said she needed to create job descriptions for various roles in the kids' ministry, one wanted to grow his ministry by a certain amount, another identified the goal of attaining a certain level of first-time guests, the youth pastor wanted to get more volunteers involved in youth camp, and so on. I asked them to break it down to what they need to accomplish in the first twelve weeks in order to stay on track to accomplish the yearly goal.

It's really about "eating an elephant one bite at a time," but there's something powerful when people have *meaningful* goals in *manageable* chunks of time. This concept isn't revolutionary, but it's very helpful to a lot of people. Those who are goal-oriented can break up the year into segments and easily identify specific goals for each time period. And those who aren't into goals aren't overwhelmed by thinking and planning for an entire year. It gives them something they can bite off and chew on. Twelve-week goals might include raising up four leaders, creating three new volunteer job descriptions, or recruiting two more volunteers. These are imminently doable!

What's the role of the pastor? To keep the cars aligned. How? By having a brief, fifteen-minute meeting with staff members each week to be sure they're staying on track for the current twelve-week period and the whole year—and encourage every step of progress. When the twelve-week year is completed, the pastor can review the year with the team members and talk about the goals for the next year. (In large churches, the executive pastor is usually the one who meets with the staff for accountability.)

I find it ironic that many people set New Year's resolutions, but by February, most of them can't even remember their goals. However, if people are focused on the next twelve weeks, it's not overwhelming. They'll not only remember; they'll accomplish them.

The entire team may have twelve-week-year goals, and each person on the team may have some or all of them on their personal lists. Shared goals keep them aligned. They will have specific goals for their departments, but also, one or two may be goals for the whole team. Let's say there are eight items on the twelve-week year—six of them are specific for the youth department or children's department, but two of them are for every staff member. This allows staff members to work on their own department's goals, but the entire team is working on specific goals as well. This ongoing exercise helps everyone make progress and move in the same direction.

The Hiring Process

After the team began to function as a more cohesive unit, and the cars were finally aligned, I told Jamal, "It's time to talk about your hiring process." Far too often, pastors of small and midsized churches—and especially pastors of churches that are growing from small to midsized—haven't thought clearly about their hiring process. They may have hired their best friend at the beginning, or maybe they inherited the entire team when they arrived. The statement applies here and throughout this book: "When desperation rises, standards fall." Many churches hire when they're desperate, and far too often, it doesn't turn out like they imagined.

WHEN DESPERATION RISES, STANDARDS FALL.

There are endless variations of how a team is formed, but each pastor has the opportunity and responsibility to hire well from that point on. Each team is, in some measure, unique, but I shared some guiding principles with Jamal and Vanessa:

1] Clarify your core values.

"Who are you no matter what?" (See the explanation of core, aspirational, and accidental values in chapter 4.) Every new hire needs to demonstrate an understanding and commitment to these values. This is where many hires derail.

2] Communicate your model of theology.

Reformed or Pentecostal, each tradition has particular angles on basic truths of the faith. One pastor was astounded when he asked a number of people the simple question, "What's the gospel?" and he got a wide range of answers, some of which weren't all that close to the truth!

3] Explain your ministry philosophy.

This is where it's easy to be vague, so work hard to find the right language to explain your perspective on the process of spiritual growth, leadership development, reporting structures, conflict resolution, schedules, and other expectations of staff members.

4] Be clear about the process.

Some pastors have told me, "Oh, I just let my executive pastor do all the hiring." I think that's a mistake. The pastor is the one who establishes the culture, and the pastor needs to be intimately involved in the hiring process. Others play their part in interviewing, discerning the fit, and making the final decision, but the pastor has to live with this person for the foreseeable future.

I explained these elements to Jamal and Vanessa, and then I let them craft their hiring process. They realized they'd hired people in the past after just one interview, and they had, to say the least, mixed results. They decided to have a much more robust process, including at least three interviews and a personality/temperament assessment. If anyone involved in the interviews didn't feel confident, they put on the brakes to slow things down until they felt they had a clear decision.

Traffic Lights

This is a simple but effective method to evaluate whether proceeding with a program makes sense. Obviously, the three lights are green (go ahead), yellow (some things still need attention before proceeding), and red (not this or not now). I work with a pastor who is one of the most visionary and high-energy leaders I've ever met, but at one point, I had to tell him, "You're killing your team! They simply can't keep up with you." I told him about this exercise and recommended he use it for every project, program, hiring decision, or expansion.

- Leadership: Do we have available, competent leaders to make it happen? Green, yellow, or red?

- Resources: Do we have the resources of money, time, space, and other materials to make it happen? Green, yellow, or red?
- Cost: Are we willing to make the sacrifices to make it happen? Green, yellow, red?
- Timing: Is this the right time, the best season, to make it happen? Green, yellow, red?

In most cases, each of these questions surfaces a number of factors, probably a dozen instead of just four. Let's say of the dozen factors, eight are green, three are yellow, and one is red. Can the one in red be overcome? Can the three in yellow be remedied? If they can, then the project is greenlit. But if five are green, four are yellow, and three are red, put on the brakes—you're not ready to move ahead.

This exercise gives a large measure of objectivity, so teams don't just assume, *Sure, things will work out!* They slow down enough to do this evaluation and determine if this is the right project, with the right resources, led by the right people, at the right time. They also have now clearly identified the roadblocks and detours so they can address them. This way, the reds and yellows can be fixed, at least well enough to move forward.

Traffic lights work for almost anything. Jamal and Vanessa used this exercise when they hired two staff members a year after their executive pastor left, and the church was growing again. Entrepreneurs can use traffic lights as a check against impulsive decisions, and more cautious leaders can use them to convince the team (and themselves) that they should move ahead.

THINK ABOUT IT:

What are some ways you can tell a team isn't aligned with the vision and values?

What is your experience with a team that is out of alignment (assuming all of us have had this experience to some extent)?

What were the consequences for the church, for the team, and for you?

Do you agree or disagree with the statement: "Healthy churches cause unhealthy people to leave, but unhealthy churches cause healthy people to leave"? Explain your answer.

What are the roles of honesty and humility in bringing a team back into alignment?

EVALUATE: Which of the exercises in this chapter might work well for you and your team?

EDUCATE: Who needs the exercises explained, so they make a difference?

ESTABLISH: What's your first step?

EXECUTE: How will you make real progress?

CHAPTER 7

FROM WOOD-FIRED TO BULLET TRAINS

P rocess. Steps. Progress. Development. We live in an "instant society" where it seems we can get almost anything from a drive-thru window, and the entire world of information is available with a few keystrokes. But the things that really matter take time.

The word *train* comes from a Latin term that means "to pull or draw." The very first trains predate steam engines by almost three centuries. Horses pulled carriages in Germany on primitive tracks in the 1500s. Modern trains came into existence with the invention of the steam engine at the turn of the nineteenth century, with the first locomotive powered by wood-fired steam debuting in England in 1804. In 1825, British engineer George Stephenson welcomed four hundred passengers to ride on his train for twenty-five miles at the startling speed of eight miles an hour. That may not impress us, but it certainly impressed people then.

In the early years, steam wasn't very efficient, and quite often, skeptics held races between horses and steam trains to show that horses were still a far better means of transportation. But steam engines improved, and by the time of the Civil War, troops and supplies were moved very efficiently in the North, which held a great advantage over the South, which had far fewer railways.

Steam engines were improved for many decades until, with the invention of the internal combustion engine powering trucks and cars in the early twentieth century, diesel power took over the rail industry. For decades, the fastest and most elegant way to travel across the country was by train, but when airlines became more popular after World War II, train travel declined precipitously. Still, the most cost-effective means to move goods was, and is, by rail.

AT EACH STAGE IN THE HISTORY OF TRAINS, CREATIVE, BOLD PEOPLE FOUND WAYS TO DO THINGS SMARTER, BETTER, AND MORE EFFECTIVELY. PASTORS CAN DO THAT TOO.

In some countries today, maglev trains move people at astonishing speeds. Maglev stands for *magnetic levitation*: the cars float on a cushion of air, suspended above the tracks, eliminating friction. China, Korea, and Japan are the leaders in this technology. A Japanese bullet train was clocked at 375 miles an hour. Visionaries in America propose using maglev on routes between major cities, but so far, they haven't figured out how to cover the cost. It's only a matter of time.

Trains are a terrific metaphor for churches, and the development of train travel gives us perspective when we face challenges that seem insurmountable. At each stage in the history of trains, creative, bold people found ways to do things smarter, better, and more effectively. Pastors can do that too.

DEMORALIZED NO MORE

I met with James, a pastor in the Midwest who felt demoralized by opposition from a few people in his church—and two of those antagonists were on his board. Over the course of about six months, he went through the process of confronting and resolving the conflict, and he began to have some hope again.

I talked with James about the scene at the end of John's gospel when Jesus restored Peter. After Jesus was arrested, Peter was humiliated and deeply ashamed when he denied Jesus three times outside the mock trial. Shame crushes the spirit, and Peter must have thought Jesus was finished with him. But He wasn't. Jesus pursued Peter and found a time for the two of them to be alone on the banks of the Sea of Galilee. There, Jesus communicated His love, His forgiveness, and a restored purpose for Peter. Jesus saw potential in Peter that Peter no longer saw, and as I shared this with James, he began to cry. He saw himself in Peter's story, and he was overwhelmed with gratitude that Jesus cared enough to restore him too.

It didn't take long for James's enthusiasm to return. His vision for growth was revitalized, and within the next year, he opened two more campuses. I talked with him recently, and he told me God had put it on his heart to start six more in the small communities around his city. He was excited about casting vision, raising money, hiring people, and seeing God do more amazing things. He told me, "Chris, I'm dreaming big dreams again!"

PUSHBACK

When I met Raymond, he told me that when he interviewed for the lead pastor role at his church, two other pastors in his denomination called him to let him know their churches were giving some money for his family to move there, but they didn't really want him to come to their city. It was such a bizarre call that he thought he'd misunderstood them. He hadn't. A few weeks after he took the position and began preaching and leading his team, he found out the two pastors were contacting people in his church to complain about him.

When Raymond reached out to me, he said, "I moved my family across the country in good faith and got a green light from the denomination, but now these two guys have been demeaning me to the state director of our denomination! I always expect opposition from unbelievers, but not this! I jumped through every hoop, and now the leader in our state is telling people I don't belong."

As the months went by and I continued to meet with Raymond to encourage him, I realized the opposition was taking a terrible toll on his leadership. As I talked with him about the people he had hired for his team, I realized he wasn't confident enough to hire stars; he only hired people who weren't as sharp, weren't as talented, and weren't as experienced as he was. He was hiring down instead of up. He wasn't hiring them because he wanted to dominate them. He was hiring them because his confidence was in the ditch, and he couldn't stand to look inferior to anyone.

I used a number of exercises with Raymond, and the lights came on. We talked about three kinds of people who may be present on staff teams: the stars, the strong and steady, and the strugglers—and the importance of hiring stars! Raymond's confidence returned, and he became the leader God created and called him to be. Recently, he hired a guy for a key position on his team. A few months later, he called me and said, "Chris, this guy is crushing it! He's doing incredible things, and people love him!"

I told him, "That's what happens when you're secure enough to hire stars."

Raymond's church outgrew the middle school where they'd met for several years. He raised a ton of money, and they're building in a prime part of their community. Raymond just needed someone to step into his life and believe in him. The two pastors who had been his antagonists have become his cheerleaders, and the denominational exec asked him to speak at the next convention.

SURPRISE

Renee is a young man who called to ask for my advice. He told me he had recently joined the team at a church of about three as an associate pastor, but only a month after he arrived with his wife and one-year-old son, the pastor abruptly announced he was leaving. It was a complete surprise, and even more surprising, the board asked him to take over as the lead pastor. When he called, he moaned, "I don't know what to do. I'm not at all sure I'm called to be the pastor. I'm really green. I feel like David showing up at Saul's army camp and being thrown into a battle with no armor and no backup. What do you think I should do?"

Like most pastors I consult with, Renee needed a big shot of encouragement, as well as some direction for his structures and strategies. I set him up with a speaking coach to help him learn how to preach, we went through some exercises to create a vibrant culture with the few staff members and key volunteers, and we spent time talking about his need for resources. That was two years ago. Today, the church has doubled in size, he has hired some terrific people, and the cash in the bank has grown from $2,000 to $100,000. The church is looking for a bigger facility, and they have real momentum.

Recently, I talked with Renee, and we recounted all that had happened since that day his pastor jumped off the train. He told me, "I know God has called me here, but it sure seems like an odd choice. Why do you think God called me to be the pastor when I was so young?"

I remembered that Renee had compared himself with David in our first conversation, so I picked up that theme. I told him, "When David arrived at Saul's camp and heard Goliath's threats, he wondered why no one was going out to fight the giant. Saul offered him armor, but it didn't fit, so

David put five stones in his bag and walked out to the field of battle. When we tell this story, we focus on the bag, but we need to focus on the basket."

Renee looked puzzled, "What do you mean?"

"David arrived that day with a basket of food for his brothers. He didn't show up ready to fight. He showed up ready to serve." I let that sink in for a few seconds, and then I said, "Renee, you showed up to serve, and God has put you in the fight."

GOD HAS CALLED YOU, HE HAS CRAFTED YOU WITH TALENTS AND EXPERIENCE, AND HE HAS PUT YOU IN THE RIGHT PLACE TO ACCOMPLISH HIS DIVINE PURPOSES.

The tools, ideas, exercises, and techniques described in this book are here for one reason: to help you serve and fight more effectively. God has called you, He has crafted you with talents and experience, and He has put you in the right place to accomplish His divine purposes. It wasn't easy for Jesus, and it hasn't been easy for leaders throughout the history of the church. We face difficulties of all kinds, but God's Spirit gives us wisdom and courage for each one. I hope the stories and exercises in this book are as useful to you as they've been for many other leaders. Use them to expand Christ's kingdom. That's what we're here for.

THINK ABOUT IT:

What are some reasons it's important to see ourselves "in process" as we learn to lead and serve?

What are the most important lessons and tools you've gotten from this book?

When and how are you going to use them? What's your first step?

APPENDIX

We've looked at a number of exercises in the chapters of this book, but there are more. Here, you'll find a list of the ones already included, so you'll know where to find them, and you'll also find some that aren't in any of the chapters.

Chapter 2
- The 90-Day Run
- The 90-Day Window
- Boxes and Batons
- Riverbanks
- Creating an Invite Culture

Chapter 3
- Follow-Up of First-Time Givers
- Follow-Up of Splash Giving
- The 90-Day Challenge
- Generosity Calendar
- Tiers of Giving
- Right, Wrong, Missing, Confusing
- Leadership Ladder
- Leadership Circles

Chapter 4
- Core, Aspirational, and Accidental Values
- Your Heart, God's Heart, and Community Needs

Chapter 5
- First Day Experience
- Quick Look
- Likable, Capable, Gravitational
- Mission Critical

Chapter 6
- Two Questions
- Matthew 18 Every Week
- 4 X 4
- 12-Week Year
- The Hiring Process
- Traffic Lights

OTHER EXERCISES

SIX PHASES

"Six Phases of a Church" is an exercise that allows the pastor and the team to evaluate the current status of the church and where it needs to go. Let me identify the phases:

The first phase is the launch. Every church has had a launch, even if it was one hundred years ago.

The second phase is utopia. Everything is going right, but most of the time, we don't know why. In reality, if you don't know why it's going right, you won't know how to fix it when it's going wrong.

The third phase is the whirlwind. If you've ever seen a tornado, you'll notice the end goes up and down. This is what happens in churches. They get into a whirlwind, their attendance goes up, but then it comes back down. It goes up again; then it comes back down, and it keeps repeating the process. The pastor and the other leaders can't figure out how to break through the ceiling. This is when you know you're in a whirlwind.

The fourth phase is when everything is up and to the right. The church is growing numerically, financially, and in every other way.

The fifth phase is a merry-go-round with a lot of movement but very little progress. At this point, churches get stuck and start to decline.

The final phase is when the church is slowly dying, but no one is willing to make the necessary changes to bring life back. Slow death doesn't happen overnight. It takes time.

The key is to identify your current phase, so you can strategize how to get to the phase of increase—and stay there. This exercise needs people to be honest about the history and the current condition of the church.

YOUR CHURCH PLAYBOOK

A clear and comprehensive playbook is important for every organization, including the church. It describes how you do church. Let's say that your church is called First Avenue Church. The playbook is "The First Avenue Way" of doing church. It includes your vision, mission, values, strategy, job descriptions, culture, etc. It describes everything you are, everything you do, and everything you hope to do in the future. Think of it this way: if everyone in the church was gone, and all that was left was the playbook, would people be able to rebuild the culture, structure, and strategy of your church based on the playbook?

I recommend that you get every department to contribute to the playbook: youth, children, groups, worship, facilities, greeters, and all other departments. Ask them to create their documents, clean them up, and make them look consistent in the branding. When you review them, make any changes, and then compile them. You'll have your playbook. If you are multisite or want to become multisite, this exercise helps new campus pastors and their teams be crystal clear about the culture and practices of the church.

The playbook will become a tool to keep everyone moving in the same direction as you continue to expand and grow.

CURB TO CHAIR

"Curb to Chair" helps you and your team understand the Sunday experience of everyone who attends your church. Of course, you're already trying to make sure guests have the best possible experience, but it's easy to make assumptions and miss some opportunities. I recommend recruiting and assigning two leaders: an inside and an outside coordinator. The outside coordinator is dedicated to everything outside the main auditorium. This person makes sure the bathrooms are clean, signage is out, music is playing in the parking lot, and everyone is in position to welcome people from the moment they turn into the parking lot until they walk through the auditorium doors to take their seats. The inside coordinator is like a Hollywood producer. This person makes sure the service is running on time, handouts are ready, the room is clean, and everything is ready to go. Evaluating the curb-to-the-chair experience is very important, and having an inside and outside coordinator will ensure a high standard of excellence.

INCREASING GENEROSITY

Every pastor wants to increase generosity among their people, and increasingly, pastors are using a strategy often known as Kingdom Builders. Here's how it works: Identify five to ten major projects you want to accomplish throughout the year. Typically, these fall into three categories: local, national, and global. You might choose some local programs like providing resources for a homeless shelter or supporting nonprofit organizations. You can partner with a national organization (or two) to help them to accomplish their mission. You're probably already involved in some kind of global outreach, but I recommend partnering more specifically with a global organization, so your people know how their money is making a difference.

At the beginning of the year, describe these projects, and ask people to make a commitment above their regular tithes. Some might commit to giving $50 or $100 per month in addition to the tithe, and others will give their yearly bonus or part of an inheritance. There are no limits to the creative ways people will give when they have a vision for the impact of their generosity! Then, throughout the year, keep people aware of progress in all the projects. At least once a month, provide a video update on one of the projects, and every week make a short progress report from the pulpit about one or more projects.

This effort could add 30 percent to the overall budget. Make sure to present it to your leaders first to get their buy-in and then to your congregation. Create a nice brochure and commitment card. The brochure will show the goals you want to accomplish locally, nationally, and globally, and people will fill out and turn in the commitment card. This isn't a "one and done" strategy—you can build on it every year. You can find out how other churches use this strategy and learn from them. Generosity changes lives—of the givers and the recipients. There are tons of resources you can find to help build this out in your church, but this will at least get you moving in the right direction.

BIG DAYS

"Big Days" are events that happen on Sundays throughout the year—days that aren't holidays such as Christmas, Easter, Mother's Day, or Father's Day. I recommend planning three or four Big Days throughout the year, attracting the interest and participation of people in your church and community. For instance, you might invite a believer who is a football player from a university to speak, or an astronaut, a scientist, or someone who has seen remarkable success in business. Big Days aren't the cornerstone of growing your church, but they provide opportunities for your people to invite their friends and neighbors to hear someone they probably wouldn't hear anywhere else. If done right, they can be big wins for your people.

INSIDE MARKETING

"Inside Marketing" is directed to people who consider your church their home. Today, the average person who is considered "a regular attender" attends church 1.7 times per month. What if you could increase that? For instance, what if you helped a person who is coming to church once every six weeks to come once a month, or someone who is coming only once a month to come twice a month? This would enable them to engage more deeply in the life of the church, and it would increase the overall attendance of the church, which would generate more momentum.

I recommend approaching this from two angles: First, the adults. At least once a month, promote the launch of a new series, entertainment in the plaza after the service, or bring in food trucks. You can also do this once a month with kids. This is the easiest and most cost-effective way to generate enthusiasm and increase involvement. Once a month, have a special day such as Superhero Sunday Splash, Sunday Reptile, Breakfast Cereal Sunday, or something else that's border-line outrageous. Creativity can be off the charts! Encourage your kids' ministry leaders to brainstorm and come up with something special every month. The student minister and the children's director can send postcards promoting the event and put a quick, handwritten note on each of the cards, such as, "Hey, Tommy, looking forward to seeing you!" Kids don't get much in the mail, so when they get these cards, they'll be excited to come to church, so they can participate in the fun!

Inside marketing isn't about reaching new people; it's about increasing the frequency of attendance of the people who go to your church already, which will give you lots of wins.

CHURCH BOOM

LEADING A CHURCH IS HARD.
WE MAKE IT EASIER.

Church BOOM's team of successful and seasoned pastors want to help you face and overcome the obstacles keeping you from experiencing explosive growth in your church.

- PERSONAL COACHING CALL OPPORTUNITIES

- VIDEO TRAINING MODULES

- FULL LIBRARY OF DOWNLOADABLE RESOURCES

- COMPLETE SERMON SERIES BRANDING PACKAGES

Learn more about Church BOOM at
CHURCHBOOM.ORG

CONNECT WITH CHRIS

Learn more about his ministry, speaking
engagements, and leadership visit

CHRISSONKSEN.COM

Chris Sonksen

@ officialchrissonksen

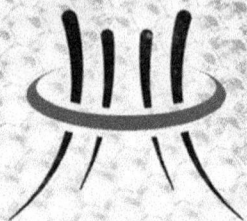

CHURCH
BOOM
ON THE WALL
PODCAST

CHURCH
BOOM
UNIVERSITY

WHEN THE PASTOR GROWS,
THE CHURCH GROWS.

growing library of
leadership masterclasses

access to live webinars with
top leadership experts

leadership resources
delivered to you door

community platform to share
and collaborate ideas